THE INTENTIONAL PARENT

Your Guide Through the 5 Dimensions of Development

Preparing Kids for LIFE

DANIEL HAGADORN

www.PK4L.com

The Intentional Parent: Your Guide Through The Five Dimensions Of Development

 PK4L Publishing
www.PK4L.com

Copyright © 2018 by Daniel M. Hagadorn

All rights reserved, including the right to reproduce this eBook or any portion thereof in any manner whatsoever. For more information, address:

Daniel Hagadorn
www.PK4L.com
dh@PK4L.com

Every attempt has been made to source all quotes properly.

ISBN: 978-0-578-19203-1

10 9 8 7 6 5 4 3 2 1

First edition, 2018

Published in the United States of America

THE PARADIGM: 360⁰ PARENTING	iii
INTRODUCTION TO USING THIS GUIDE	1
THE TOP TWO FEARS THAT EVERY PARENT HAS	7
Introduction	9
Fear №1: "I'm not qualified"	12
Fear №2: "I'm going to mess up my kids"	17
Truth №1: You are the "gatekeeper"	21
Truth №2: You are the "interpreter"	24
THE SEVEN LESSONS YOU NEVER KNEW YOU LEARNED IN SCHOOL	27
Introduction	29
Lesson №1: Confusion is the new normal	35
Lesson №2: Know your place in the food chain	37
Lesson №3: Nothing important happens in class	39
Lesson №4: Your will isn't yours	41
Lesson №5: Your mind isn't yours	43
Lesson №6: Self-esteem trumps learning	45
Lesson №7: Your privacy isn't yours	47
Recommended Resources	50
DE-SCHOOLING IN SIX SIMPLE (but not easy) STEPS	53
Introduction	55

TABLE OF CONTENTS

Step №1: Start with the right source	60
Step №2: Believe you are fully equipped	62
Step №3: Socialize your children	64
Step №4: Educate sons & daughters differently	67
Step №5: Just do your best…period	71
Step №6: Never forget the "WHY"	73
Recommended Resources	77
THE FIVE KEYS TO SUCCESSFUL MENTORSHIP	79
Introduction	81
Key №1: Envision	83
Key №2: Encourage	85
Key №3: Empower	88
Key №4: Extend	90
Key №5: Emphasize	92
Recommended Resources	95
SCHOOLING VS. EDUCATION: A brief history	97
THE NEW PARADIGM OF EDUCATION	107
A NEW CURRICULUM	123
QUESTIONS: Sections 1-9	129

THE PARADIGM: 360 PARENTING

360º PARENTING

We use the term **360º Parenting** to describe the process of engaging your child in all five dimensions of human development to empower…

1. Their *learning*…which happens everywhere, and at all times.
2. Their *time*…because every moment, can be a teachable moment.

THE FIVE DIMENSIONS OF DEVELOPMENT

- ❏ Spiritual
- ❏ Emotional
- ❏ Mental
- ❏ Social
- ❏ Physical

THE THREE STAGES OF LEARNING

- ❏ Download
- ❏ Organize
- ❏ Synthesize

THE THREE STYLES OF LEARNING

- ❏ Visual
- ❏ Auditory
- ❏ Kinesthetic

THE FOUR PERSONALITY TYPES

- ❏ Sanguine | Extrovert
- ❏ Phlegmatic | Introvert
- ❏ Choleric | Extrovert
- ❏ Melancholic | Introvert

THE PARADIGM: 360 PARENTING

An Interconnected Network

The framework of 360º Parenting is designed to support parents in helping their children become fully prepared for life as the best version of themselves. Understanding and applying this framework empowers you to fully engage your children in each of the five dimensions of human development to help them become everything they were meant to be.

- ❑ Spiritual
- ❑ Emotional
- ❑ Mental
- ❑ Physical
- ❑ Social

Each dimension has its own distinguishing characteristics, and they all interconnect and overlap with one another.

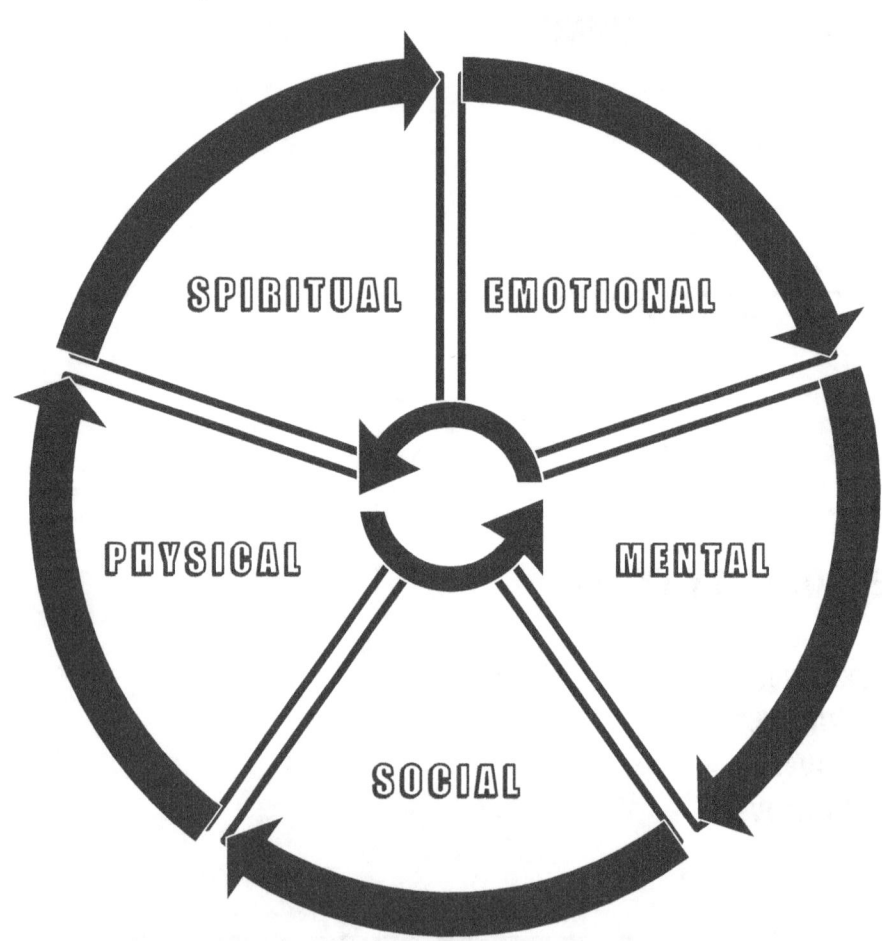

THE PARADIGM: 360 PARENTING

The Three Stages Of Learning

Understanding that all learning happens in three stages* will help parents more effectively engage their children in each of the five dimensions of development.

*NOTE: Every child is unique, and the ages below provide a reference point, not an exact line of demarcation for their development.

- ❏ **Grammar** (ages 1-10) – absorbing information.
- ❏ **Logic** (ages 11-13) – sorting information.
- ❏ **Rhetoric** (ages 14-18) – applying information.

Perhaps the use of gardening metaphors might be the best way to illustrate the learning process...

- ❏ **Grammar I Download**. Parents prepare the "soil" of their children's hearts and minds by sowing and watering the "seeds" of knowledge.

- ❏ **Logic I Organize**. Parents continue to cultivate the "soil" and pot the "sprouts" of understanding to promote healthy growth.

- ❏ **Rhetoric I Synthesize**. Parents re-plant the "saplings" of wisdom into cultivated "soil" outside of the pots. As these "roots" deepen over time, the "branches" require less and less parental "pruning" to maximize overall growth.

Collectively, the three stages of learning can also be explained as three gates that *everyone* must pass through...but *each in their own manner*. Walking, running, crawling, jumping, skipping...or on a pogo stick. ☺

Having an awareness of what learning stage a child is operating in enables parents to set realistic expectations for their progress. This greatly reduces the potential for frustration (both theirs and the child's) while creating the best possible environment for developing a "love of learning" and "learning how to learn."

THE PARADIGM: 360 PARENTING

THE 3 STAGES OF LEARNING

DOWNLOAD | AGES 1-10

sowing — watering

ORGANIZE | AGES 11-13

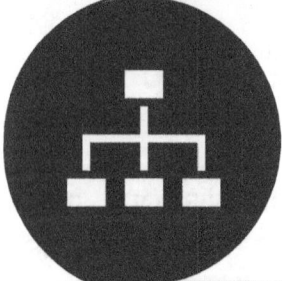  

cultivating — potting

SYNTHESIZE | AGES 14-18

re-planting — pruning

THE PARADIGM: 360 PARENTING

Building On The Stages Of Learning

To maximize a child's progress through each of the **three stages of learning**, their preferred **style of sensory learning** must be considered as well. The three primary styles are…

- **Visual**…a child processes information through what they see (e.g., written word, picture images, graphs, charts, maps, and diagrams).

- **Auditory**…a child processes information through what they hear: listening, speaking (e.g., lectures, group discussions, oral reports, and mnemonics).

- **Kinesthetic**…a child processes information through physical experience (e.g., hands-on, activity-driven, practical connections to the real world).

The ancient sage Confucius (551BC-479BC) might have described sensory learning styles this way, "I hear, and I forget, I see, and I remember, I do, and I understand."

Although your child *can* and *should* operate in **ALL** three learning styles (and there are even multiple variations within these three), they will almost certainly have *a preferred style of learning*.

Connecting with your child in their preferred learning style helps them to navigate each of the three stages of learning more effectively and will dramatically improve their level of *comprehension*.

So, as you engage your child in each of the five dimensions of development…

As you navigate with greater confidence through the three stages of learning…

Your ability to communicate in their preferred learning style will be significantly enhanced by understanding their temperament, or personality type.

THE PARADIGM: 360 PARENTING

THE 3 STYLES OF LEARNING

VISUAL

written word   images

AUDITORY

speaking   listening

KINESTHETIC

hands-on   activity

THE PARADIGM: 360 PARENTING

Translating The Language Of Personality

There are four basic temperaments, or personality types (some even include a fifth, Supine), and each type has its own unique characteristics, strengths, weaknesses, and motivators. While it is impossible to neatly fit all of humanity into only four categories, there are endless variations within each of the four. This is just a starting point and represents a "doorway" into who people are.

- **Sanguine (extrovert)**
- **Phlegmatic (introvert)**
- **Melancholic (introvert)**
- **Choleric (extrovert)**

The personality types can be better understood as "languages." Therefore, the more "fluent" a parent becomes in their child's "language", the better they will communicate. Alternatively, "illiteracy" can make things much more difficult. Imagine telling someone the exact geographic location of $1 million...but in Chinese (not helpful, unless, of course, you speak Chinese). ☺

Although everyone has *each of the four* personality types to varying degrees, everyone also has both a *primary* and *secondary* type. Therefore, identifying a child's primary and secondary type is the first step towards becoming "fluent" in their "language."

"Fluency" will:

- Enable you to communicate more effectively.

- Help you to know *when and how* to appropriately apply encouragement and correction.

- Equip you with the necessary motivators to cultivate their strengths and train their weaknesses (i.e., undirected strengths).

These principles form the foundation from which to experiment with all of the wonderfully different methods, techniques, and applications (i.e., practical's) unique to your child that will help them become their best.

THE PARADIGM: 360 PARENTING

THE 4 PERSONALITY TYPES

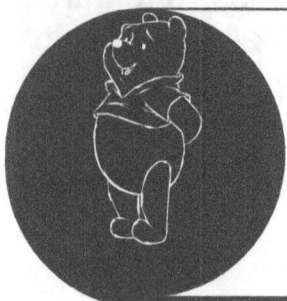
SANGUINE
Extrovert

WINNIE THE POOH

PHLEGMATIC
Introvert

PIGLET

MELANCHOLIC
Introvert

RABBIT

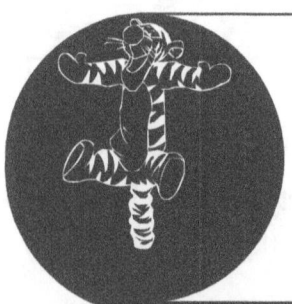
CHOLERIC
Extrovert

TIGGER

THE PARADIGM: 360 PARENTING

At this point, you are likely having one of two reactions.

1. "I finally have a map and am ready for the journey ahead!"

2. "I feel totally overwhelmed."

Or maybe you find yourself somewhere in between. Regardless of where you are, understanding the difference between **principles** and **practicals** will help. A lot.

Principles = time-tested ideas that universally apply to everyone.

Practicals = ideas that work well for individuals, or for particular situations.

At PK4L, we only focus on **principles** because they remain as true today as they were in the past, and as they will be in the future.

But **practicals** are developed over time as they are progressively adapted to the individual, or to the situation and require *two things*:

1. *Patience.* (It takes time to figure out the best ways to help your child).
2. *Grace.* (Not everything works out the way you hope it will).

Experimenting to figure out what's best for your child is *a process that happens over time.* You keep what works, discard what doesn't, and just keep going.

However, since even the most well-intentioned experiments don't always work out the way we hope, we must be willing to learn from our mistakes without self-condemnation. (Hint: easier said than done ☺).

Ultimately, this process begins by:

❏ Acknowledging our fears.
❏ Identifying the source of those fears.
❏ Removing those fears.
❏ Replacing those fears with time-tested principles of success.
❏ Putting it all into consistent practice.

THE PARADIGM: 360 PARENTING

notes

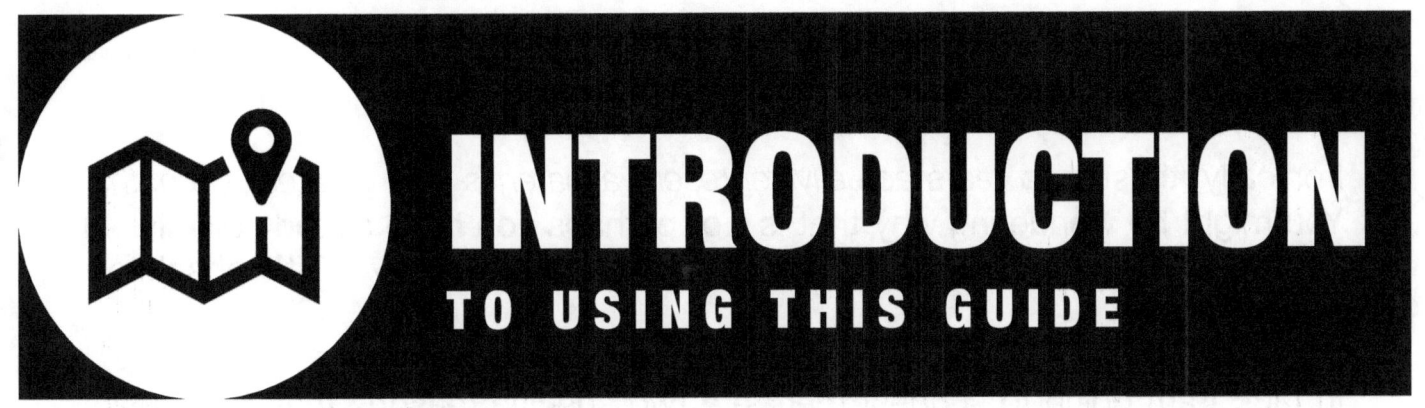

INTRODUCTION
TO USING THIS GUIDE

I am one of those people fortunate enough to truly love what they do. The joy of teaching high school since 2002. The blessing of homeschooling our daughter since 2008. The honor of speaking at numerous educational conferences. In their own way, each of these experiences have made me even more grateful for the life I have.

However, since beginning this journey, something has always troubled me…even to this very day. Something about parents.

It never ceases to amaze me how often parents sell themselves short…*even though they love their children more than anyone else on the planet and no one is more committed to their children's success*.

But, if that's true, then *why do parents often think, feel, and act as though someone else would do a better job than they would*? Then, one day, the answer suddenly came to me in an unexpected "a-ha" moment.

You see, over the last 20+ years, parents have asked me A LOT of questions. At back-to-school nights, at parent-teacher conferences, and Q&A sessions at speaking events. It would be fair to say that at least 95% of those questions were really **fears masquerading as questions**. And those fears are the direct result of **our own schooling**.

Collectively, their questions revealed the two greatest fears that every parent has about preparing their kids for life…

1. **"I am not qualified."**

2. **"I am going to mess up my kid(s)."**

INTRODUCTION TO USING THIS GUIDE

Ironically, these two fears *actually represent a parent's two greatest strengths.* You might be wondering why that is…or perhaps you have already dismissed that statement as "blowing sunshine." But let me assure you, it's absolutely true.

In fact, I am going to suggest there are two specific reasons that these fears affect almost *every* parent…

1. **The deep love we have for our children leaves us extremely vulnerable to insecurity, doubt, and anxiety concerning what is best for them.**

2. **We have been schooled to rely upon "experts" to tell us what is best for our own children, instead of trusting ourselves (i.e., the ones who love our kids the most).**

But what if you could *intentionally* direct your children's future *with confidence*? Secure in the knowledge that you were the best qualified and that you would not mess them up? What would that feel like?

Well, just like everything in life, there is a way that things work. In three steps. **Enlighten. Equip. Empower.**

Enlighten. (*The Seven Lessons You Never Knew You Learned in School*). The first step is to identify the lessons that we never knew we learned in school. Our teachers never lectured about it. We were never tested on it. We never read about them in any of our textbooks.

But, after spending seven hours a day, five days a week, forty weeks a year, for thirteen years…we learned these lessons *very, very, well*.

The whole process is actually quite insidious because how do you know what you don't know? It's sort of like explaining what it means to be wet…*to a fish*. They don't know any different since it's all they have ever known. Similarly, we don't know any other way to think about learning than the way we have been taught to think about schooling.

INTRODUCTION TO USING THIS GUIDE

Equip. (*De-schooling in Six (but not easy) Steps*). After we've identified these harmful lessons, we can begin step two: *scrubbing them from our minds*. This process must continue until the "lessons" no longer interfere with our perspective…and ultimately, the choices we make to prepare our kids for life.

For example, if you decided to repaint your living room, you would prepare the walls by filling in the holes and cracks and sanding all the surfaces. Then, you would apply a coat of primer and begin painting. The process of "de-schooling" works exactly the same way.

Empower. (*The Five Keys to Successful Mentorship*). Lastly, if we don't replace these harmful lessons with the right ones, we will eventually default to the way of thinking that caused so much insecurity, doubt, and anxiety in the first place. However, once free of these "lessons", we will be empowered to mentor our children into the very best version of themselves.

After all, no one loves your children more than you do. No one is more committed to their success. No one knows them as well as you do. How they learn. How they are motivated. Their likes and dislikes.

In fact, YOU are the number one expert on your own children and whatever you *intentionally* decide concerning their future…is going to be the *right choice*.

But…if preparing our kids for life is a journey, then we better make sure we're navigating with the right map…or else we'll just end up lost.

Imagine you're in Austin, Texas, with only a map of Los Angeles, California to guide you. How frustrating would that be? You're wandering aimlessly, trying to find your way using a map that has no relevance to your current location.

It's not just confusing…it's counterproductive.

You might try changing your behavior. To dedicate yourself to *working harder* and with *greater diligence*. But you would just get lost faster.

INTRODUCTION TO USING THIS GUIDE

You might try *changing your attitude*. To become more optimistic and to think positively. But you would still be lost. [You might just have a better attitude about it].

Only when you have the correct map of your location does diligence and optimism become important...or even useful. *But neither of these two virtues can overcome following the wrong map.*

So, let's take a moment to consider some **"What IF's."**

What IF...

We stopped following the edutocracy's mass-produced, standardized path to "success" and took the "road less traveled" instead?

What IF...

Our children were no longer wasting their time reflexively regurgitating a series of pre-determined answers absorbed during K-12 schooling and were taught how to "learn how to learn" and think for themselves instead?

What IF...

Parents experienced the glorious joy of helping their children embrace their God-given talents and pursue their passions with relentless enthusiasm?

What IF...

Parents confidently empowered their children to become their best so that they would be fully prepared to step into God's design for their lives?

I don't pretend to know all the answers (who does?)...but I have been living and researching them for several years now, and in the pages that follow, I will share with you everything I have learned so far.

INTRODUCTION TO USING THIS GUIDE

This is a quick preview of the five sections we will be going through together...

1) The Top Two Fears That Every Parent Has

Discover. *Why every parent's two greatest fears are actually every parent's two greatest strengths.*

2) The Seven Lessons You Never Knew You Learned In School

Enlighten. *Identify the lessons you never knew you learned in school to discover where those two fears came from.*

3) De-Schooling in Six Simple (but not easy) Steps

Equip. *Clear those lessons from your mind to ensure that they no longer interfere with how you choose to prepare your kids for life.*

4) The Five Keys To Successful Mentorship

Empower. *Apply time-tested principles of mentorship to replace those lessons and empower your child to become the very best version of themselves.*

5) Knowledge APPLIED is power

Begin. *The secret of getting better, is getting started. Apply what you've learned one step and one question at a time.*

INTRODUCTION TO USING THIS GUIDE

notes

THE TOP TWO FEARS THAT EVERY PARENT HAS
& why they are really your *greatest strengths*

- ❏ FEAR № 1: "I'm not qualified"
- ❏ FEAR № 2: "I'm going to mess up my kids"
- ❏ TRUTH № 1: You are the "gatekeeper"
- ❏ TRUTH № 2: You are the "interpreter"

E³ Enlightened. Equipped. Empowered.

THE TOP TWO FEARS THAT EVERY PARENT HAS
& why they are really your *greatest strengths*

- ❏ **FEAR № 1:** "I'm not qualified"
- ❏ **FEAR № 2:** "I'm going to mess up my kids"
- ❏ **TRUTH № 1:** You are the "gatekeeper"
- ❏ **TRUTH № 2:** You are the "interpreter"

E³ Enlightened. Equipped. Empowered.

INTRODUCTION

As parents, there is no sacrifice we wouldn't make for our children...which is exactly why we are so vulnerable to doubt and insecurity about whether we really *are* doing the best for them. But we cannot afford to allow our insecurities to become the "lens" through which we see ourselves or raise our kids.

So, what if you could be *certain*? What if, instead of being fearful, you could feel *confident* about the decisions you make concerning your children's future? Would you want to know how?

To spare you some suspense, the short answer is **intentionality**...which I define as being clearly informed about your options when deciding what is best for your children.

- ❏ **THE PARENT decides WHERE their children are educated.**

- ❏ **THE PARENT decides HOW their children will be educated.**

- ❏ **THE PARENT decides BY WHOM their children will be educated.**

INTRODUCTION

Since we only have so much time to make a difference in the lives of our children...the importance of being intentional cannot be overstated.

In fact, consider this question for a moment...*what has the greatest influence on your child?*

I'm going to suggest that the answer is **time**. It is a fact of life that time will be spent...but our intentions determine whether time promotes us...or exposes us.

Disclaimer: My wife and I have homeschooled our daughter since 2008, and we believe that it was the best way for our family to be intentional about her education...but it's certainly not the only way. In fact, parents today have any number of wonderfully innovative options available to them.

Regardless of where, how, or from whom...our children are ALWAYS learning...for better or worse.

So, the most important question is really this: how involved will we choose to be in the process of preparing them for life? Because in the end, our choices must *be intentional*.

Parents can always be counted upon to choose the best for their children...*the real quesion is this: "What information will they rely upon to make those choices?"*

So, after all my years in education...after fielding countless questions from parents...the two questions that recycled themselves over and over again, both took the form of, "I don't have what it takes to be a good parent."

INTRODUCTION

Though asked a number of different ways, these two questions were basically two *fears* driven by two *lies*...

☞ I am not qualified.

☞ I am going to mess up my kids.

Although you may doubt your "qualifications"—*the truth is,* there is literally no one else on planet earth who loves your child more than you do...which makes you *the most qualified* to raise your child.

Although you may worry whether you're going to "mess up your kids"—*the truth is,* God knew exactly what He was doing by entrusting YOU with the care, training, and education of His child.

It should also be noted that both of these fears are almost entirely the result of our own schooling...

    Seven hours a day...
        Five days a week...
             Forty weeks a year...
                For thirteen years.

So, instead of relying upon our God-given curiosity to spark our interests and inspire the pursuit of knowledge...we were trained to depend upon so-called "experts" to tell us what to think about *everything*...including parenting.

The reality is that children never discover their best by default. Consequently, helping your child become their best requires two commitments:

1. **Being intentional about their education and training.**

2. **Embracing your God-given role as the number one expert on your own children.**

FEAR N⁰ 1
"I'm not qualified"

And before we go further, just remember who you are...*the number one expert on your own children*. So, can I just pause a moment to point this out?

YOU. ARE. A. HERO.

There is no doubt that raising children is challenging...*but it's also amazing beyond description*. Unfortunately, there are no red-carpet, internationally-televised award shows that honor and celebrate parenting (although there should be).

Nevertheless, does it even need to be said that it takes *far more courage to be intentional*...day after day...year after year...in the life of a child than it does to play a parent on TV?

The fear that causes you to doubt your parenting abilities is exactly why it's so important to see things differently. For example, if we looked through blue-lensed sunglasses, *everything would look blue.* In the same way, whenever we look through the wrong "lens," our vision of parenting becomes "colored" by that lens.

When our vision is distorted, the tyranny of the immediate rules over the important. These choices accumulate over time and make it increasingly difficult to change the "lens."

And the older we are, the more lenses we have coloring our perceptions.

FEAR №1: I'm not qualified

However, to really address this first fear, we must do more than just change the lens...we must *choose* to see ourselves and our role as parents the same way that God does.

Once we embrace the conviction that we have been "pre-qualified" by Him, our experience of intentional parenting starts to change.

The Apostle Luke likewise affirmed the importance of carefully choosing one's teacher saying, **"A disciple is not above his teacher, but everyone when he is fully trained will be like his teacher."**

It's quite clear that the fulfillment of a child's potential is either limited, or expanded, according to who has taught them. And who is better qualified than the parent to make that decision?

> It's supposed to be hard. If it wasn't hard, everyone would do it. The hard...is what makes it great.
> — JIMMY DUGAN, *A League of Their Own*

I love this quote because the challenge of parenting *literally* proves the greatness of the endeavor. What a relief! You are doing something great...*so of course it is challenging.*

The truth is...YOU are the only one who knows what it feels like to walk a mile in your shoes. And since everyone experiences their life at 100%...I can only imagine with what's it like to walk in yours.

However, please allow me to offer this encouragement: *never let the challenge diminish the importance of what you're doing.* It matters. While there's no question the road isn't easy, NEVER doubt that *you are farther along than you think...* ☺

***Disclaimer: It is not my intention here to soapbox against teachers or the school system, but I REFUSE to allow parents to experience even one

FEAR №1: I'm not qualified

moment of insecurity for not having a piece of paper "certifying" their ability to direct the course of their children's education. As someone who has been "certified" since 2002, please hear me… **The. Paper. Means. Nothing.*****

Consider for a moment, who we consider "experts" and how often these experts have gotten it wrong…sometimes *very* wrong.

- In 1899, Charles Duell, U.S. Patent Commissioner, said, **"Everything that can be invented, has been invented."**

- In 1943, Thomas Watson, Chairman of IBM, said, **"I think there is a world market for maybe five computers."**

- In 1962, Dick Rowe, Head of A&R at Decca Records, said, **"[rejecting The Beatles] Not to mince words, Mr. Epstein [the Beatles' manager], but we don't like your boys…and guitar groups are on their way out."**

- In 1999, a Mars orbiter designed for NASA by Lockheed Martin was lost in space due to a simple math error. Lockeed engineers used English measurements while the NASA team used metric ones. The discrepancy led to a malfunction of the *$125 million ($233 million 2023 USD)* spacecraft and *the probe was lost*.

So… "experts" like these are more qualified than you to know what is best for your own children?

Yes, legitimate experts exist, but we have set the bar rather low and have overused this title into near meaninglessness.

FEAR №1: I'm not qualified

- No teacher...no matter how many awards they have won...no matter how committed they are...will ever out-love or out-dedicate you when it comes to your own children.

- Even the *best teacher's* attention is divided among 20-45 students per class, and they usually teach at least five classes of students. So, your child is receiving somewhere between $1/110^{th}$ and $1/225^{th}$ of their attention while attending class.

The only reason Monopoly® money doesn't fool anybody is because we already know what real money looks like. So, once you understand and embrace the truth about your qualifications...anyone claiming to be an "expert" on your own children suddenly loses their credibility.

However, IF our "lens" is distorted...THEN it becomes much harder to tell the difference between real money and Monopoly® money.

But here is the difference...

YOU are striving to help your children discover their best so that they will be fully prepared for life...*the school system is not*.

Instead, the school system is designed to mass-produce students to think and behave predictably...with standardized testing being the clearest example of this sort of flawed thinking.

FEAR Nº1: I'm not qualified

notes

FEAR No 2
"I'm going to mess up my kids"

Now that you know how qualified you REALLY are, let's address the second fear. Remember…

> **1** **Your children are a gift from God and He doesn't make mistakes. That fact alone, makes you more than qualified.**
>
> **2** **We have been trained to rely upon "experts" to tell us what to think about everything…but they will never know our kids as completely, or love them as deeply, as we do. Which is exactly why you are not "messing up" your kids.**

It's important to hold on to this perspective moving forward…

King David of Israel wrote, **"Don't you see that children are God's best gift? The fruit of the womb his generous legacy?"**

His sentiments are echoed in the Apostle Paul's letter to the Ephesians, **"For we are God's masterpiece."**

Children are God's most precious gift to parents, and we have been given the great privilege of helping our sons and daughters become who their Creator intends them to be. But the greatest obstacle preventing parents from embracing this reality is *fear*.

Since fear and faith cannot exist together in the same space, intentionality obligates you to decide which one will occupy that place in your mind.

The good news, as psychiatrist Karl Augustus Menninger (1893-1990) reminds us, is that **"Fears are educated into us, and can, if we wish, be educated out."**

FEAR №2: I'm going to mess up my kids

When fear goes unchecked, the words of King David, the Apostle Paul, and Dr. Menninger become little more than warm-fuzzy clichés and we quickly default to *looking through the wrong lens...which only serves to magnify our fears completely out of proportion.*

Fortunately, we have been given a daily reset button...because not every day goes according to plan. [As you've probably already noticed ☺].

Simply allow yourself to enjoy the freedom of what you likely never experienced when you were in school...

❑ the love of learning.
❑ the meaningful engagement of the mind.
❑ the discovery and development of your God-given design.

Remember: no one is more committed to your child's success than you are! That fact alone should reassure you that won't mess up your child. Will you make mistakes? Of course. Who doesn't? But you are always training two generations at a time...yours and theirs. Enjoy the process! In the end, the best lesson you can impart to your children is *a love of learning* and the *ability to self-educate*.

> Those who know how to think need no teachers.
> — MOHANDAS GANDHI (1869-1948)

Besides, no human being has ever truly "taught" another human being anything. It's like when you learned to ride a bicycle. Advice. Guidance. Modeling. Encouragement. Absolutely.

But ultimately, *you just needed an environment that empowered you to teach yourself.* It is no different with our children. They just need to learn how to teach themselves while being mentored into excellence...instead of being standardized into predictable compliance.

FEAR №2: I'm going to mess up my kids

In light of our rapidly changing world, possessing the ability to "learn-how-to-learn" is an absolutely priceless skill.

Take a moment to consider the legacy you want to leave behind for your children. Whatever that legacy is...*I can guarantee that it wasn't inspired by school, or a textbook, or a standardized test.*

For example, this is the legacy I want leave behind for my daughter...

- ❏ **To have a passionate love for God, others, and life in general.**
- ❏ **To have the ability to self-educate.**
- ❏ **To discover and fully embrace God's design for her life.**

Each of us have been given an incredible story to live...but if we choose not to step into our own...*our children will have greater difficulty discovering theirs*.

Accepting that your greatest fears as a parent are actually your greatest strengths...empowers you to become confidently intentional about the decisions you make concerning your children's future.

> Children are the living messages we send to a time we will not see.
> —NEIL POSTMAN (1931-2003)

FEAR №2: I'm going to mess up my kids

notes

TRUTH Nº1
You are the "gatekeeper"

Time, once it has been spent, is gone forever. Although you can always make more money…you cannot buy more time. (And if you have ever lost a loved one, you know better than most just how valuable time is…what wouldn't we give for just one more hour of time with them?)

Since time can *only be spent, never saved,* we must carefully consider **how** we are spending time with our kids.

K-12 113,880

Kindergarten through 12th grade consumes 113,880 hours of a child's life. During that time, they will spend…

- ❏ 37,960 hours sleeping = 33%
- ❏ 35,590 hours on media (low estimate) = 31%
- ❏ 18,200 hours in school = 16%
- ❏ 4,160 hours doing homework = 4%
- ❏ 17,970 hours with friends + extracurriculars + meals + family = 16%

TRUTH №1: You are the "gatekeeper"

Since parents are basically sharing that tiny slice of *17,970 hours (16%) with friends, extracurricular activities, and meals*...that doesn't exactly leave very much time to help their kids navigate life...much less build a legacy for their future.

Quoting Dr. Daniel Levitin, popular economist Malcolm Gladwell noted...

> 10,000 hours of practice is required to achieve the level of mastery associated with being a world-class expert in—ANYTHING.
>
> —DR. DANIEL LEVITIN

And every year, 4.5 million students graduate from high school as world-class experts in...?

I don't know about you, but I sure wasn't a world-class expert in *anything* after graduating from high school.

Fortunately, parents don't have to wonder what could have been accomplished with that time. As the gatekeeper, moms and dads can *choose to be intentional* about how they spend that time with their children.

Being The Gatekeeper

This simply means there is no outside influence that doesn't go through you first. You decide what, and who, is allowed inside your children's lives.

Ultimately, you are training them to develop healthy boundaries and equipping them for the day when they decide for themselves what influences will be allowed into their own lives.

TRUTH №1: You are the "gatekeeper"

notes

TRUTH №2
You are the "interpreter"

In addition to being the gatekeeper, you are also the interpreter. This means framing everything that enters your children's lives into the proper context. After all, as your children absorb the world around them, whose lens do you want them looking through? Yours? Or someone else's?

For example, whenever they fall short of the mark, *help them interpret the difference between failing and failure.*

FAILING
= diligence + excellence of effort

--- vs ---

FAILURE
= quitting and/or mediocre effort

TRUTH №2: You are the "interpreter"

IF your child did their best...

1) Failing enables the discovery of what *does not work.*

2) And that discovery results in experiencing the freedom to figure out what *does work.*

Since that which is rewarded...gets repeated, children eventually learn to value *excellence of effort over results.* Consequently, failing will be understood as the quickest path to achievement. And ultimately, a proper understanding of failing + excellence of effort *will produce results.*

Remember...

As the parent, you are the most qualified person to 1) translate the language of personal success into the lives of your children and 2) empower them to become the very best version of themselves.

- **YOU are the number one expert on your own children because no one knows them better than YOU do.**

- **There is no one more qualified than YOU to determine your children's path forward because no one is more committed than YOU to their success.**

- **Yes, EVERYONE makes mistakes, BUT YOU love your children far too much to "mess them up" because YOU are more motivated than anyone else to correct those mistakes.**

THE TOP TWO FEARS...

notes

THE SEVEN LESSONS YOU NEVER KNEW YOU LEARNED IN SCHOOL

- ❏ **LESSON № 1:** Confusion is the new normal
- ❏ **LESSON № 2:** Know your place in the food chain
- ❏ **LESSON № 3:** Nothing important happens in class
- ❏ **LESSON № 4:** Your will isn't yours
- ❏ **LESSON № 5:** Your mind isn't yours
- ❏ **LESSON № 6:** Self-esteem trumps learning
- ❏ **LESSON № 7:** Your privacy isn't yours

E³ — Enlightened. Equipped. Empowered.

THE SEVEN LESSONS YOU NEVER KNEW YOU LEARNED IN SCHOOL

- ☐ **LESSON Nº 1:** Confusion is the new normal
- ☐ **LESSON Nº 2:** Know your place in the food chain
- ☐ **LESSON Nº 3:** Nothing important happens in class
- ☐ **LESSON Nº 4:** Your will isn't yours
- ☐ **LESSON Nº 5:** Your mind isn't yours
- ☐ **LESSON Nº 6:** Self-esteem trumps learning
- ☐ **LESSON Nº 7:** Your privacy isn't yours

E³ Enlightened. Equipped. Empowered.

INTRODUCTION

Our compulsory government school system is perhaps one of America's greatest "success" stories. Sound ridiculous? Consider this: in all my years of teaching AP/College Prep U.S. History, World History, Government, Economics, and Geography in public/private high schools...and even among my fellow teachers, students, and their parents...*almost no one could imagine educating students any differently.*

Over 100 years ago, the government monopoly of compulsory schooling became America's new educational paradigm...and even now, only a handful of educators can envision any other alternative.

After all my years of classroom experience, I have come to share John Taylor Gatto's conviction that the **method** of schooling is the only real content it teaches. And that's precisely why the redemption of America's compulsory school system cannot be accomplished through "improved" curricula, equipment, or teachers.

As Gatto wisely notes, if we want our children to experience true education, then they should be learning to:

- ❑ **learn how to learn,**
- ❑ **serve others and a higher purpose than just themselves,**
- ❑ **love from the heart,**
- ❑ **persevere,**
- ❑ **be courageous, and**
- ❑ **be honorable**

INTRODUCTION

Needless to say, the school system fails to address any of these essential building blocks of individual potential.

For instance, "critical thinking" was an oft-repeated buzzword that echoed through every staff development or teacher in-service I ever attended; it always promised a brighter tomorrow for our students. And it certainly would…**IF** it were ever actually implemented.

However, any school that dared to equip their students with the tools that develop free minds would not last a year without completely collapsing on itself…so don't hold your breath.

In fact, delegating the training of students to "certified experts" has *prevented* our children from developing into their fullest potential. If that assessment seems harsh, consider the compulsory school system's latest product, *the Millennial (and now GenZ) generation…*

INTRODUCTION

① **Millennials are largely indifferent to adult responsibilities, the future, and nearly everything…except the diversion of toys and violence.**

② **Regardless of socio-economic status, Millennials find it difficult to concentrate on anything for very long.**

③ **Millennials possess a poor sense of historical context and their individual place within it.**

④ **Millennials are mistrustful of intimacy like the children of divorce they really are [and often "divorced" from meaningful parental engagement].**

⑤ **Millennials despise solitude, are entitled, materialistic, dependent, passive, violent, timid when confronting the unexpected, and addicted to distraction.**

For purpose of conversation, Millennials are described here in admittedly generalized terms.

Clearly, the issues confronting Millennials require a very different approach than the one being offered by the edutocracy…which is why the current debate concerning national curriculums (Common Core® is just the latest incarnation) is complete nonsense.

A national curriculum has existed for quite some time and is already deeply embedded in the *seven lessons you never knew you learned in school.*

Moreover, the national hysteria over our failing academic performance completely misses the point.

INTRODUCTION

Schools teach *exactly* what they were designed to teach, and they do it *exceptionally well*:

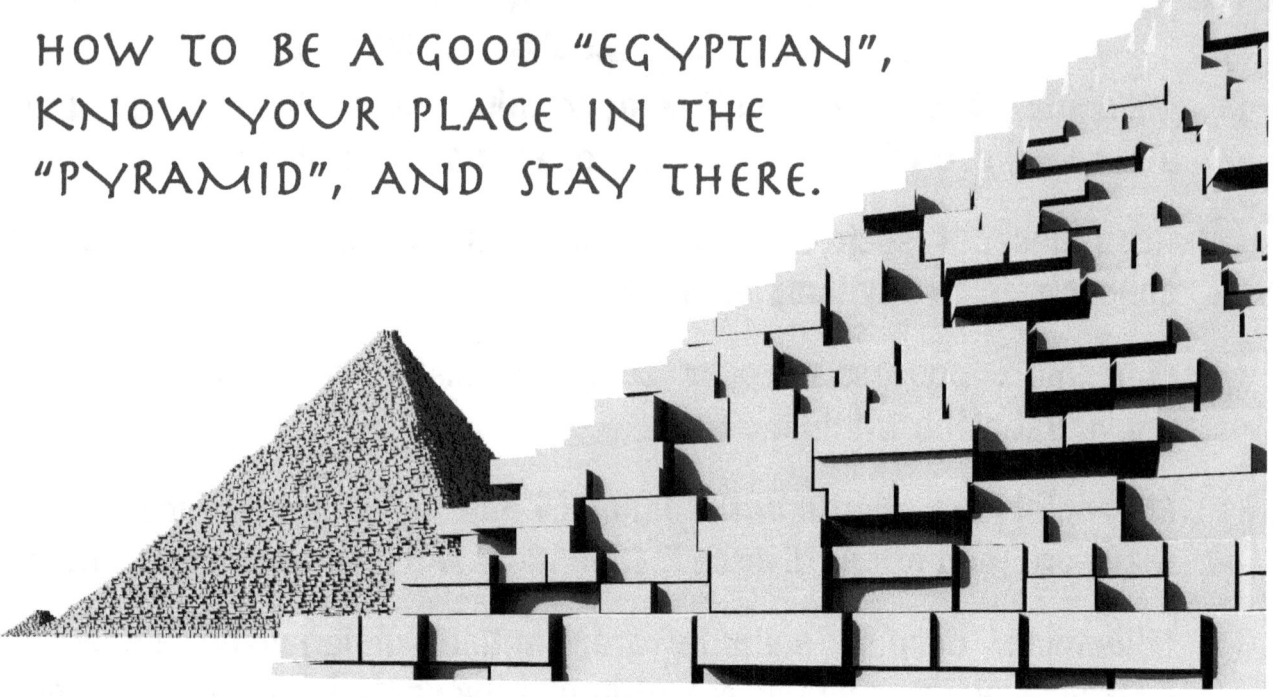

HOW TO BE A GOOD "EGYPTIAN", KNOW YOUR PLACE IN THE "PYRAMID", AND STAY THERE.

To be fair to Millennials (and now GenZers), at least they're beginning to understand that graduating from college with $100K of debt and a double major in Marxist Pottery and Selective Outrage didn't make them more employable.

It's worth remembering that only a few generations ago, life in general, and education in particular, *was very different in the United States*. Back then, originality, variety, and self-sufficiency were the currency of the times.

These ideals gifted our country with a freedom that made us the envy of the civilized world; social-class boundaries were easily crossed, and our citizenry was marvelously confident, innovative, and intellectually independent.

Somehow, we accomplished this all by ourselves without large-scale government intrusion, and without institutions and social agencies instructing us how to think and feel.

INTRODUCTION

But the reach of centralized social control expanded considerably during the Civil War and has moved inexorably into our modern era. Before this development, education was offered to whatever degree an individual desired...*because only centralized societies require a government monopoly of compulsory school systems to maintain themselves.*

People learned to read, write, and compute arithmetic quite well with some studies even suggesting that literacy at the time of the American Revolution (at least for non-slaves on the Eastern seaboard) was close to 100 percent. For instance, Thomas Paine's Common Sense sold 600,000 copies to a population of 3,000,000—20% of whom were slaves, and 50% were indentured servants.

In fact, a 5th-grade math or rhetoric textbook from 1850 would likely be considered college level today. If you need factual reassurance of this, read Benjamin Franklin's *Autobiography*, which reveals an innovative man of great intellectual and moral understanding who had no time to waste being schooled.

The depth of Franklin's education exposes another serious error in the edutocracy's paradigm, namely that "professional teaching" actually causes things that are inherently easy to learn (e.g., reading, writing, and arithmetic) to become difficult to learn by insisting they be taught by "experts" using standardized pedagogical methods.

INTRODUCTION

> If we regained a philosophy that locates meaning where meaning is genuinely to be found—[in God], in families, in friends, in the passage of seasons, in nature, in simple ceremonies and rituals, in curiosity, generosity, compassion, and service to others, in a decent independence and privacy, in all the free and inexpensive things out of which real families, real friends and real communities are built—then we would be so self-sufficient we would not even need the material 'sufficiency' which our global 'experts' are so insistent we be concerned about.
>
> — JOHN TAYLOR GATTO

These are the sort of lessons that cannot be learned in school because they are simply not taught there. School is very much like starting life with a 13-year jail sentence in which bad habits are the only curriculum. Sadly, I observed these habits being taught in every classroom…*even the best ones.*

There is absolutely no doubt that without the benefit of reading Mr. Gatto's books, I would have taught each and every one of these seven lessons to my own students…*sincerely believing that it was for their benefit.*

It is a sad truth that there has been greater harm done in the name of sincerity than in the name of tyranny.

The Seven Lessons You Never Knew You Learned in School is an architectural blueprint for constructing the machine that "produce[s] and maintain[s] a permanent underclass" of people forever deprived of discovering and experiencing their highest potential.

LESSON №1
Confusion is the new normal

Public schools teach...

- ❑ Curriculum without a context.
- ❑ Curriculum that is un-related to other subjects.
- ❑ Curriculum that is based upon disconnected information and activities.

Public schools—even the best ones...

- ❑ Exploit a student's inability to coherently address the panic and anger they experience from these constant violations of natural learning sequences.

- ❑ Graduate students with an arsenal of superficial jargon derived from a variety of subjects that they have been trained to value...instead of graduating students with a genuine enthusiasm for learning.

- ❑ Sell this process to both children and parents as "quality education."

NOTE: I polled my students on this issue every year and they consistently reported that their enthusiasm for learning almost always ended by 6th- or 7th-grade...largely because they struggled to make sense of what they were supposed to be learning (even the ones who "did all the work and aced all the tests.")

The Problem...

Human beings instinctively seek genuine meaning in their learning, not a series of disconnected subjects and facts that seldom seem related to each other.

- ❑ True education involves in-depth, inter-connected learning, an experience rarely, if ever, enjoyed in public schools.

LESSON №1: Confusion is the new normal

❑ The edutocracy has developed a seemingly random network of "learning" sequences that are further distorted by their obsession with unproven educational fads that obstruct and confuse the normal process of learning.

Thus, *confusion is forced upon students* "by too many strange adults, each working alone with only the thinnest relationship with each other, pretending for the most part, to an expertise they do not possess."

QUESTIONS TO PONDER

① How many teachers do you really think are willing to entrust their students with the tools of critical thought inside of an institution that demands unquestioning obedience/acceptance?

② How much of what you "learned" in school can you even remember today?

③ Based on whatever you can remember, how much of what you "learned" do you consider valuable?

LESSON N⁰ 2
Know your place in the food chain

Schools create an impersonal environment between teachers and students...

❑ Students were placed on my class roster without any explanation why (and the edutocracy made it is crystal clear that it was none of my concern).

❑ Every student was properly numbered; and the methods for numbering students increased dramatically during my fourteen-year teaching career.

❑ My internal email correspondence eventually required that a student's name be replaced with their six-digit school ID number. (This was just one of several obstacles to valuing and appreciating the human being underneath the numbers).

❑ Numbering and ranking children is an enormously profitable business [just ask the College Board®], though the purpose of that business remains a matter of debate.

As a teacher my expected "responsibilities" were...

❑ To make sure students "liked" their classroom confinement...or, at the minimum, endured it.

❑ To support the edutocracy in their efforts to promote envy and fear of the "higher" classes [AP and Honors] and contempt for the "lower" classes [Special Ed, ELL, ESL].

❑ To use school, just like every other rigged competition, to teach students to "accept their place."

LESSON №2: Know your place in the food chain

The Truth Behind The Labels

Categorization is always sold as being for the "benefit" of the child [Special Ed/ELL/ESL/ICAP programs are cash cows for schools and so are PSAT/SAT/ACT/AP prep classes] *even though it has the opposite effect.*

This is why I relentlessly exposed my students to the charade of "education" and the abysmal results it has produced. I simply gave them the "keys to the factory" and allowed them to observe the process of "making sausage."

At the end of the day, I just tried as hard as I could, for as long as I could, to help as many as I could…and still wish that I could have done more.

① In general, did you feel valued by your teacher(s)?

② Was your personal potential developed…or neglected?

③ If you were fortunate enough to have a great teacher, what set them apart from the others?

LESSON Nº3
Nothing important happens in class

For an edutocracy to function properly...

❏ Students must be encouraged to cultivate the "virtue" of indifference while pretending that they actually care a great deal about the subject.

❏ Teachers must demand "total engagement" in the lesson while students energetically compete with one another for the teacher's favor.

For my part...

❏ I made every effort to clearly define the line between *actual learning* and *state-mandated "busy work"* for my students.

❏ But I was also forced to invest considerable time and effort into "lesson planning" to produce this required pretense of student "enthusiasm" in order to avoid being fired.

The True Function Of The School Bell

Bells essentially served two functions:

❏ To condition students to automatically stop working on their assignments and proceed immediately to the next workstation. (Which completely ignores how children actually learn things).

❏ To obliterate important contexts—like the past or the future—by transforming every classroom minute into mind-numbing sameness, and "inoculat[ing] each undertaking with indifference."

LESSON №3: Nothing important happens in class

Remember Pavlov's dogs? Children have been treated as lab experiments for far too long. And school bells are just part of the "research."

Consequently, the two most powerful lessons the compulsory government school system teaches to their students (and reinforces with bells)…

 No work is worth finishing…and even if it was, nothing important will ever be finished in the classroom, so why bother caring too much about anything you do there?

 No student should ever receive a complete educational experience but should instead treat classes like an academic "payment plan"…that never actually pays off.

QUESTIONS TO PONDER

① How much of modern schooling is based upon passing a standardized test or regurgitating whatever the teacher and/or textbook says is true…and how much is based actual learning?

② How much "educational conditioning" have we carried forward into our lives today?

LESSON №4
Your will isn't yours

Conditioning Emotional Dependency

This is instilled in children (K-12), by giving students…

❑ happy faces, gold stars, and red checks.
❑ smiles and frowns.
❑ prizes and public correction.
❑ GPA's and class rankings.

These methods…

❑ break and condition the students' will.
❑ force them to acknowledge the "proper" chain of command.

CONDITIONING IS NOT EDUCATION

LESSON №4: Your will isn't yours

What Personal Rights?

Once "properly conditioned," students accept that their rights are *solely dependent upon the will of the authority*.

❏ Their rights may be granted or withheld—without appeal—because rights do not exist inside a school.

❏ Even the Supreme Court has ruled that school authorities may define, limit, or suspend a student's right to free speech.

The Teacher's Role

Teachers exercise and reinforce this **authority** in a variety of ways:

❏ Deciding who is issued a bathroom pass.
❏ Initiating a disciplinary action to address behavior that threatens their control.
❏ …And even when teachers know that students are not really "going to the bathroom" but give the pass anyway, students are still being conditioned to depend upon the teachers' **favor**.

Privileges that can be extended or withdrawn effectively transform students into **hostages** for "good" behavior.

Instead of encouraging capable students to challenge themselves or helping struggling students to improve…the "good" of the class [collective] is placed above all other considerations.

Individuality, something deeply valued by children and teenagers, is suppressed at every opportunity.

So…is the system educating children, or training and herding sheep?

LESSON № 5
Your mind isn't yours

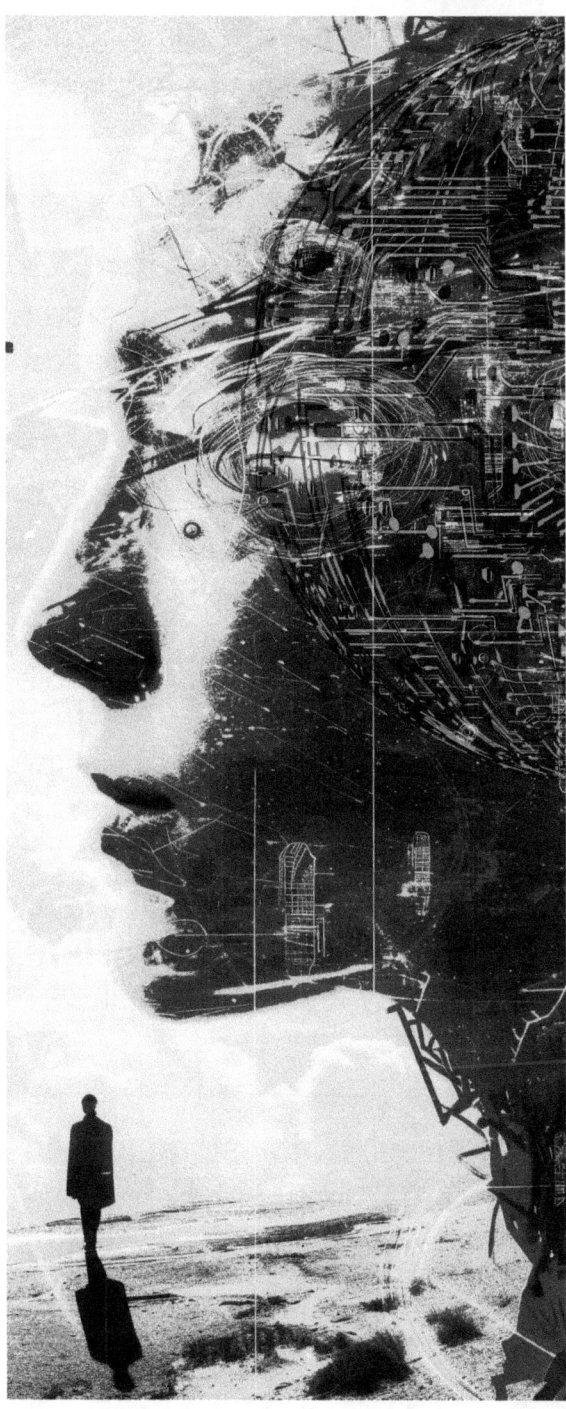

First Personal Will, Then The Mind

"Good" students are programmed to wait for their teachers to tell them exactly what to do and think. Thus, students are trained to rely on "experts"…

- ❏ to establish meaning for their lives,
- ❏ to make all their important choices, and
- ❏ to validate those choices.

…And then, the edutocracy determines the curriculum that the teacher will force their students to study.

The "Good" Student…

Performs their assigned tasks with a minimum of resistance and a reasonable show of enthusiasm.

- ❏ Intellectual or behavioral "deviants" [read: independent thinkers, or those who are simply fed up with having their time wasted] must be publicly punished as a warning to others.

- ❏ This process allows teachers to easily identify and separate "successful" students from the "failures."

LESSON №5: Your mind isn't yours

Finite Options = Finite Learning

Although there are literally millions of important and interesting things to study, the edutocracy would have us believe that *they alone* possess the requisite expertise to decide which topics the student will study...*and which they will not study.*

Thus, schooling reinforces *conformity over curiosity* [if there is even a place for curiosity in our schools anymore].

Just A Thought

How many businesses would literally go bankrupt if the school system didn't force students to surrender their minds? How much of our economy is based upon this foundational ideal?

- What would happen to the social-service industry without "mindless consumers?"
- What would happen to school counselors and therapists without "a steady supply of emotional invalids?"
- What would happen to commercial entertainment of all sorts, including media, if we discovered how to create our own fun?
- What would happen to "restaurants, prepared-food and a whole host of other assorted food services if people returned to making their own meals rather than depending on strangers to plant, pick, chop, and cook for them?"
- What would happen to much of modern law, medicine, the clothing industry, and even teaching without a "guaranteed supply of helpless people" that continue to pour out of our schools every year?

> **The school system has been conditioning the masses into standardized compliance for well over 100 years now. Consequently, people have become habituated to doing whatever they are told because they no longer know how to tell themselves what to do. After all, if you don't think for yourself, someone else will always be happy to think for you.**

LESSON №6
Self-esteem trumps learning

The reward for conformity is that everyone likes you but yourself.

The Curse Of Conformity

When children become convinced that they are unconditionally loved…that they are valued for who they truly are…the resulting self-confidence inoculates them against the pressure to conform and empowers them to confidently step into their God-given design.

But to prevent this, the edutocracy makes every effort to promote counterfeit versions of self-esteem.

Their efforts have had nearly the opposite effect as children are now growing up with *lower* self-esteem than previous generations.

LESSON №6: Self-esteem trumps learning

The Method To Their Madness

How long would our modern society survive a steady stream of confident high school graduates?

- ❏ The school system intervenes as early as possible to ensure that a child's self-esteem depends upon "expert" opinion.

- ❏ Consequently, students are placed under continuous assault from evaluations, assessments, and standardized tests.

- ❏ Every five weeks, a "progress report" is sent home to officially record a teacher's approval/disapproval down to a single percentage point.

- ❏ These grades inform parents precisely how satisfied/dissatisfied they should be with their children.

Ironically, the cumulative weight of these "objective" evaluations forces children to view themselves and their futures in a very pre-determined way…yet parents would be stunned to discover how little time and reflection teachers actually devote to recording these scores.

The Evaluation That Matters

Self-evaluation has been the cornerstone of every major philosophical system that has ever appeared on planet Earth.

- ❏ The true lesson of tests, grades, report cards, GPA's, and class ranks is that children should never trust themselves or their parents…*but should instead rely on the evaluation of certified "experts."*

- ❏ After all, without grades and certified experts, how else could anyone know whether anything has been "learned."

> Every child has been gifted with their own unique form of genius. The only question left to answer is…how will you help them cultivate that gift?

LESSON Nº7
Your privacy isn't yours

What Does Surveillance Have To Do With Education?

Students are under constant observation from the moment they set foot on campus until the moment they leave.

❑ These observations are conducted by teachers, administrators, deans, and even their fellow students [often with the assistance of social media].

❑ Students are only allowed 430 seconds to move from one class to the next, 15 minutes for nutrition and 35 minutes for lunch…in order to minimize meaningful social interaction.

❑ Students are encouraged to snitch on each other and on their own parents. And parents are likewise encouraged to detail their own children's disobedience because the family that snitches together…is unlikely to resist the edutocracy's agenda.

The "Value" Of Homework

Homework is a form of "soft surveillance" that inserts itself into the household and prevents students from using their free time for "unauthorized learning", such as…

❑ Learning from a parent.
❑ Learning from personal exploration.
❑ Learning from some form of apprenticeship/internship.

LESSON №7: Your privacy isn't yours

Thus, schooling extends its all-seeing reach far beyond the final bell.

The Lesson Learned

No one can be trusted, and privacy is illegitimate. As Gatto insightfully notes:

> Surveillance is an ancient imperative, espoused by certain influential thinkers, a central prescription set down in **The Republic** [Plato], in **The City of God** [Augustine], in the **Institutes of the Christian Religion** [Calvin] in **New Atlantis** [Bacon], in **Leviathan** [Hobbes], and in a host of other places. [The] childless men who wrote these books [all arrived at the same conclusion]: children must be closely watched if you want to keep a society under tight central control.
> — JOHN TAYLOR GATTO

Children are meant to follow their own drummer...unless you force them to join a uniformed marching band and play an instrument they don't like.

THE SEVEN LESSONS...

notes

RECOMMENDED RESOURCES

JOHN TAYLOR GATTO

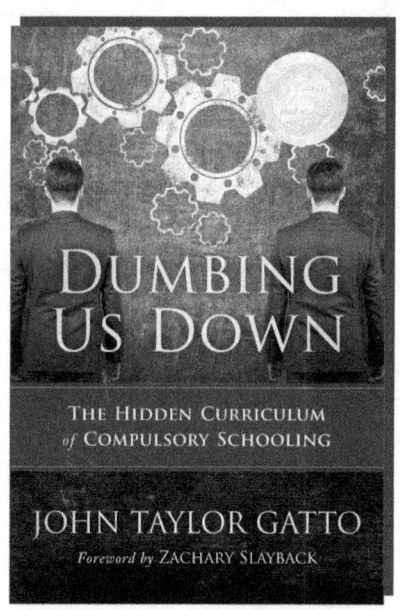

RECOMMENDED RESOURCES

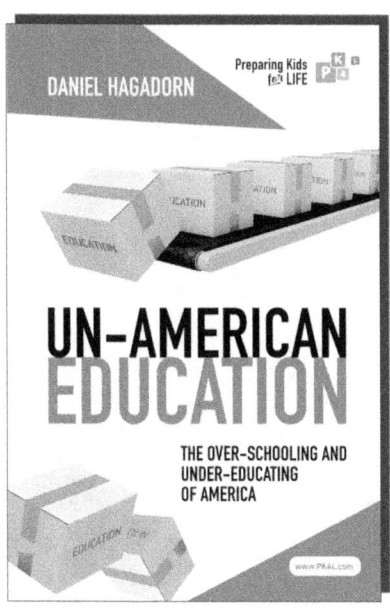

RECOMMENDED RESOURCES

DE-SCHOOLING IN SIX SIMPLE (but not easy) STEPS

- STEP № 1: Start with the right source
- STEP № 2: Believe you are fully equipped
- STEP № 3: Socialize your children
- STEP № 4: Educate sons & daughters differently
- STEP № 5: Just do your best...period
- STEP № 6: Never forget the "WHY"

E³ ➤ Enlightened. Equipped. Empowered.

DE-SCHOOLING IN SIX SIMPLE (but not easy) STEPS

- ☐ STEP № 1: Start with the right source
- ☐ STEP № 2: Believe you are fully equipped
- ☐ STEP № 3: Socialize your children
- ☐ STEP № 4: Educate sons & daughters differently
- ☐ STEP № 5: Just do your best...period
- ☐ STEP № 6: Never forget the "WHY"

E³ ➤ Enlightened. Equipped. Empowered.

INTRODUCTION

As the section heading suggests, the six-steps to de-schooling are indeed quite simple, but the process is far from easy. For example, losing weight may be a simple matter of healthy exercise and proper nutritional management…*but would anyone really describe the process as easy?*

Like any unhealthy habit, the longer we practiced it, the more effort and patience will be required to correct it. In some ways, it's sort of like explaining the concept of "wet" to a fish.

We don't know any other way to be educated than how we were taught—how could we?

INTRODUCTION

Consequently, when we choose to become intentional about the education of our children...the process can be quite challenging to implement [insert understatement here]. Thus, while we educate our children, we are simultaneously de-schooling ourselves.

So please take a moment, right now, to cut yourself a giant piece of slack, especially since you were almost certainly a product of the "system."

Much like The Matrix, America's compulsory government school system represents the paradigm we have been "plugged" into...leaving most people either unaware or unwilling to disconnect from a self-destructive but comfortably familiar form of schooling.

That said, I would never presume to tell you how to educate your child for one very important reason. Your children are not my children. If I could do a better job of raising them, God would have given them to me instead of to you.

Since He never makes mistakes, that means you have been equipped to teach your children something *they can only learn from you*. While I can offer you the benefit of fourteen years of classroom experience and the results of years of extensive research, I don't know the first thing about educating *your* child.

However, and I say this emphatically, **how** you prepare your child for life is of the utmost importance because **training = discipleship.** And discipleship is not to be done by default...it requires intentionality, thoughtfulness, and a clear purpose.

INTRODUCTION

As I mentioned earlier, whenever I have spoken at educational conferences, or even have general conversations with people about education, there are always questions...*lots of questions*.

And it would be fair to estimate that at least 95% of these questions relate to problems linked to our own schooling.

Of that 95%, the overwhelming majority of questions can be summarized as, "I don't have what it takes to be a good parent."

Homeschoolers (my wife and I included), are frequently asked if we are worried about ruining our children's futures by teaching them ourselves.

Permit me to answer that question with another question:

"So, you're suggesting that the public schools we attended made us so stupid and incompetent that we are now incapable of educating our own children? And if so, why would we voluntarily choose to send our own kids into that same system?"

Take a moment to recall your own experiences from public or private high school...what do you remember that still matters today? As Dorothy Sayers wisely noted in her provocative essay, "The Lost Tools of Learning" (1947):

> **Do you ever find that young people, when they have left school, not only forget most of what they have learned (that is only to be expected), but forget also, or betray that they have never really known, how to tackle a new subject for themselves?**
> — DOROTHY SAYERS (1893-1957)

INTRODUCTION

Most of us were "institutionalized" by the school system. Like Brooks—the elderly prison inmate from **Shawshank Redemption**—whose inability to embrace his freedom after serving a 50-year sentence ended in tragedy. The school system steals freedom from both teachers and students in precisely the same way.

As a teacher, I was continually surprised by how many of my students seemed incapable of accepting, or even understanding, the freedom I offered them in class.

Considering the 18,200 hours spent in school (K-12), we should have vast reservoirs of knowledge and expertise at our mental fingertips...right?

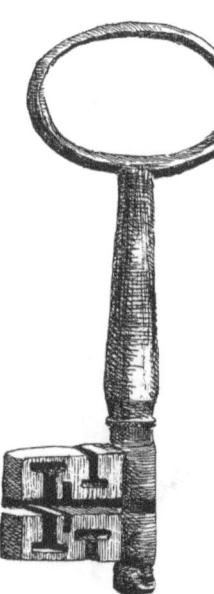

After all, as famed economist Malcolm Gladwell (*Outliers, 2008*) illustrated with the **"10,000-hour rule"**, studies have proven the key to becoming a *world-class expert in anything* is largely a matter of practicing/studying a specific task for 10,000 hours.

So, after being schooled for 18,200 hours, we should have graduated from high school with at least one—and very nearly two—"key(s)" to success. But did we? Is that how you would describe your high school experience? Or do you just have some faded photos of yourself dressed in a cap-and-gown and holding a diploma?

INTRODUCTION

PONDER THIS...

What actual doors of success did that 18,200-hour "key" open for you? And if all those hours failed to help you discover and develop your highest potential, then what exactly was the point?

The school system literally steals time from students. Precious time that would be far better spent pursuing their God-given talents and passions.

If your child was given the time...just imagine what they could do with it...

When we choose to be intentional about preparing our kids for life, it quickly becomes evident that we are simultaneously educating two generations at a time—theirs and ours.

My **schooling** ended at graduation...but my **education** began immediately thereafter. Recalling the words of Nobel Prize-winning Irish playwright George Bernard Shaw:

> The only time my education was interrupted was when I was in school...My schooling not only failed to teach me what it professed to be teaching but prevented me from being educated to an extent which infuriates me when I think of all I might have learned at home by myself.
>
> —GEORGE BERNARD SHAW (1856-1950)

STEP №1
Start with the right source

Insights To Consider

Parents have been blessed with both the capacity and the responsibility for discipling their own children. Ultimately, who do you want your children to be like…you…*or their teachers*?

- Time will either promote or expose the value of what our children learn (K-12, 7 hours a day, 5 days a week, 40 weeks a year, for 13 years = 18,200 hours).
- The **quality** of a mentor/educator in a student's life is of immeasurable importance.
- Are we intentionally preparing our children for their best life?

Every child is an image-bearer of God, and the life of every child holds so much potential that thoughtful consideration is warranted when making decisions concerning their future.

- If you send your children to "Caesar" [the compulsory school system] to be mentored/educated, they will come back "Romans."
- "Who, or what will have the greatest influence in the life of my child?" is the most important question for a parent to ask.

Evidence To Consider

The widespread use of education+propaganda aggressively proselytizes on behalf of secular humanism.

- The focus of this propaganda grooms both students and parents to adopt a predictably standardized way of thinking.
- This way of thinking excludes God and affirms the "divinity" of humanity.

STEP №1: Start with the right source

For example, Charles F. Potter (1885-1962):[1]

- Advisor to Clarence Darrow in the Scopes Trial (1925).
- Founder of the First Humanist Society of New York (1929)--whose advisory board included Julian Huxley, John Dewey, Albert Einstein, and Thomas Mann et. al.
- One of the original 34 signatories (incl. Dewey) of the First Humanist Manifesto in 1933.
- Founder of the Euthanasia Society of America in 1938.

> Education is thus a most powerful ally of humanism, and every American school is a school of humanism. What can a theistic Sunday school's meeting for an hour once a week and teaching only a fraction of the children do to stem the tide of the five-day program of humanistic teaching?
> — CHARLES F. POTTER (1885-1962)

I will let others judge the moral effect of this on society, but the academic impact has been painfully obvious.

Consider...the 50 states—including Washington, DC—and the federal government collectively spent $23,574 (2015 USD) per student, per year to produce:[2] [3] [4]

- **A national literacy rate of 88%.**
- **A national high school graduation rate of 75.5%.**
- **A national drop out rate of 4.1%.**
- **A national reading proficiency of only 41.8%.**
- **A national mathematics proficiency of just 32.2%.**

---

[1] Charles Francis Potter, *Humanism: A New Religion* (New York, NY: Simon & Schuster, 1930), p. 128.
[2] www.nces.ed.gov/pubs2011/2011312.pdf.
[3] www.cia.gov/library/publications/the-world-factbook/fields/2103.html#xx.
[4] www.hks.harvard.edu/pepg/PDF/Papers/PEPG11-03_GloballyChallenged.pdf.

STEP №2
Believe you are fully equipped

The Myth Of The "Trained Professional"

The *majority of teachers are genuinely caring individuals who deeply desire to make a positive difference in the lives of their students*, but tenure has granted the profession immunity from responsible oversight.

❑ Teaching credentials have **nothing** to do with being a good teacher and are a complete waste of time...says I, the "trained professional" who has enjoyed 20+ successful years of teaching high school.

Whenever parents feel even a hint of insecurity or inadequacy about being intentional in mentoring/educating their own children, consider this:

❑ High school graduates who intended to major in education[1] scored in the bottom third of the SAT compared to 36 other intended majors.

❑ Nationally, these education majors finished 25th out of 36 in reading, 27th out of 36 in math, and a combined 57 points below the national average SAT score in both.

❑ For example, a high school social studies teacher who earns a BA degree in Education will graduate with fewer units in social studies than someone who earned an AA degree in Social Studies.

❑ Teachers also posted dreadfully low scores on the 2011-2012 Graduate Record Examinations (GRE).

---

[1] Ron Matus, "SAT scores of teacher wannabes", *Tampa Bay Times* (2 September 2008). www.nmu.edu/philosophy/sites/DrupalPhilosophy/files/UserFiles/GRE_by_Intended_Major_2012_Data.pdf

STEP №2: Believe you are fully equipped

No teacher, no matter how caring, no matter how many degrees they have, no matter how professionally decorated…will ever care about your child, and your child's success in life, more than you do. Period.

① What causes you to doubt that God has equipped you to be intentional concerning how your children are educated?

② What, if any, insecurity do you have about being the number one expert on your own child? Why?

STEP №3
Socialize your children

How Does Society Socialize Children?

Alcohol[1]

Youth Risk Behavior Survey (2011) found that among high school students during the past 30 days...

- 39% drank some amount of alcohol.
- 22% binge drank.
- 8% drove after drinking alcohol.
- 24% rode with a driver who had been drinking alcohol.

National Survey on Drug Use & Health (2011) found that...

- 25% of youth aged 12 to 20 years drink alcohol.
- 16% reported binge drinking.

Monitoring the Future Survey (2011) found that...

- 33% of 8th graders and 70% of 12th graders had tried alcohol.
- 13% of 8th graders and 40% of 12th graders drank during the past month.

Drugs[2]

- In 2013, 7% of 8th graders, 18% of 10th graders, and 23% of 12th graders used marijuana in the previous month.
- In 2013, 15% of 12th graders used a prescription drug non-medically.

---

[1] www.cdc.gov/alcohol/fact-sheets/underage-drinking.htm
[2] www.drugabuse.gov/publications/drugfacts/high-school-youth-trends

STEP №3: Socialize your children

Sex[3]

❏ Young people ages 15-25 contract 19 million STDs annually.
❏ Two young people ages 13-29 contract HIV every hour.

Social Issues

As a teacher, as a parent, and as a member of society, I've experienced "the village"…and I certainly don't want it raising my daughter.

❏ Parents are the rightful **gatekeepers** and **interpreters** of ALL social issues for their own children according to their own values…NOT the educrats who run the compulsory government school system (or anyone else for that matter).

Team Sports

While there is nothing inherently wrong with team sports, they should be placed in proper perspective.

❏ Although sports CAN be a beneficial experience for your child, A LOT depends upon the coaching philosophy and the character of both your coach and your teammates.

If our children learn…

❏ How to love from the heart
❏ How to honor and respect others
❏ How to make and keep friends
❏ How to remain resilient in the face of adversity
❏ How to remain true to their convictions without becoming self-righteous or hypocritical

…they will do just fine in the socialization department.

---

[3] www.nationalsafeplace.org/safe-place-teens/sex-pregnancy/

STEP №3: Socialize your children

QUESTIONS TO PONDER

① Do the men and women with the best character and highest virtue usually play professional team sports?

② Are these men and women the "heroes" that we want our children to emulate?

③ When did sitting at a desk in an age-segregated classroom divided into six periods of 53 minutes each, and interrupted by 15 minutes for nutrition, and 35 minutes for lunch = being "socialized" into the "real world?"

STEP №4
Educate sons & daughters differently

Some Differences To Consider

Although we all have the same **value** before God, it is a biological fact that men and women are physically, emotionally, and mentally **different**. It only harms our children to pretend otherwise.

- ❑ The school system teaches our sons and daughters as though they are interchangeably identical—*despite the wealth of bio-psychiatric studies demonstrating their intrinsic differences*. However, the best way to help children realize their potential is by taking into account the child's individual temperament, inclinations, interests, strengths, weaknesses, *and genders*.

How Boys And Girls Learn Differently

There are gender-specific personality traits which affect how children learn despite the fashionable assumption that gender differences in personality are "socially constructed." For instance, on average, younger boys and girls demonstrate significant differences (e.g., "How long can you sit still, be quiet, and pay attention?") in their classroom behavior.

- ❑ These differences remain as they become older but become more subtly defined.

- ❑ According to the National Institutes of Health (NIH) these differences remain consistent across all cultures.

- ❑ Girls typically perform better than boys academically but are more likely to be overly self-critical in evaluating their academic performance.

- ❑ Boys typically have an unrealistically high estimate of their own academic abilities and accomplishments.

STEP №4: Educate sons & daughters differently

Motivating Boys And Girls G-E-N-E-R-A-L-L-Y Speaking

****Yes, there will *always* be exceptions to *every* rule.****

For example: the paradox of the girl who gets straight A's but thinks she's stupid and feels discouraged vs. the boy who's barely getting C's but thinks he's brilliant.

GIRLS

- Actively encourage the girls and build them up.

- Girls are motivated by pleasing adults (e.g., parents & teachers).

BOYS

- Offer the boys a reality check to help them understand they're not as brilliant as they think they are and challenge them to do better.

- Boys are motivated by studying material that interests them.

Overcoming Academic Struggles

GIRLS

- Girls usually interpret their failures as proof they have disappointed an adult, and thus, they are of little worth.

- Girls tend to view the teacher as an ally and will often welcome the teacher's help with a little encouragement.

BOYS

- Boys usually view their failures as relevant only to the specific subject area in which they have failed.

- Boys usually just want to know that their time is not being wasted.

STEP №4: Educate sons & daughters differently

- Context enhances learning for most girls, but often just bores most boys.

- Even the environments are different. For example, a girl-friendly learning environment would be safe, comfortable, and welcoming (e.g., a sofa and some comfortable bean bags, addressing the teacher by their first name).

Learning New Things

- For example: Teaching girls a new song would begin with why the composer wrote the piece, who it was written for, or a personal story about how you messed up your solo at the school talent show...*while boys just want to learn the song already.*

- For example: Teaching math to girls should be relevant and connect what they are learning to the real world...*while boys are more stimulated by focusing on the various properties and functions of numbers, even abstract ideas.*

Of course, there are ALWAYS exceptions, but exceptions DO NOT disprove the rule.

Remember, there are absolutely NO differences in WHAT girls and boys CAN learn. But there are significant differences in HOW they learn.

References:
1. Paul Costa, Antonio Terracciano, & Robert McCrae, "Gender differences in personality traits across cultures: robust and surprising findings," *Journal of Personality & Social Psychology*, Vol. 81, No. 2, pp. 322-331.
2. Alan Feingold, "Gender differences in personality: a meta-analysis," *Psychological Bulletin*, Vol. 116 (1994), pp. 429-456.
3. Diane Ruble, "The role of gender-related processes in the development of sex differences in self-evaluation and depression," *Journal of Affective Disorders*, Vol. 29 (1993), pp. 97-128.
4. Eva Pomerantz, Ellen Altermatt, & Jill Saxon, "Making the grade but feeling distressed: gender differences in academic performance and internal distress," *Journal of Educational Psychology*, Vol. 94, No. 2 (2002), pp. 396-404.
5. Eva Pomerantz & Jill Saxon, "Conceptions of ability as stable and self-evaluative processes: a longitudinal examination," *Child Development*, Vol. 72 (2001), pp. 152-173.

STEP № 4: Educate sons & daughters differently

QUESTIONS TO PONDER

① Do you consider the gender of your child when mentoring, educating, and training them?

② What changes can you make to personalize their learning?

STEP №5
Just do your best...period

Learning vs. Schooling

Standardized tests are designed to demonstrate what a student DOES NOT know, rather than what they DO know.

- "Acing" a test does not necessarily mean that learning has occurred.
- The usual "learning" pattern for most students is cram→ace→forget.
- When you can teach something in simple terms to another person...THEN you have learned.

Are Grades The Best Metric For Learning?

- What does an "A" mean to a student who IS a "good test taker," but hasn't really learned the subject?
- What does a "C" mean to a student who studies diligently and comprehends the subject, but ISN'T a "good test taker"?

True learning happens when your child understands that...

1. The object of learning is NOT the completion of "busy work" or getting "good grades."
2. The ONLY learning expectation is: "Did you do your best?"
3. IF they have done their best, then it doesn't matter how far "ahead/behind" they are in the "curriculum."
4. Success is defined by the *excellence of their effort,* not the result.
5. There are only two objectives: (1) **to love learning** + (2) **learn-how-to-learn**.

Then, and only then, will a child be truly engaged in meaningful education as they are being prepared for life as the best version of themselves.

STEP №5: Just do your best...period

Preparing For The Future

❑ Consider this: the Top Ten in-demand jobs of 2010 did not even exist in 2004.

❑ By the age of 38, the average worker will have held 14 jobs.

❑ Learning-how-to-learn is the *only* way to successfully access and apply new knowledge in order to thrive in a rapidly changing environment.

❑ *Once a child learn to self-educate*, there will be no human endeavor that excludes them.

??????????? QUESTIONS TO PONDER

① If you had a $100 million to invest, which of the following two candidates would you hire to manage the money?

❑ **Summa Cum Laude at Harvard University who graduated top of their class from the Wharton School of Business.**

❑ **High school graduate who spent the last eight years being personally mentored in finance/investment by famed investor Warren Buffett (net worth: $65+ billion).**

STEP Nº 6
Never forget the "WHY."

The Problem And The Challenge

The compulsory school system mass-produces predictably standardized intellectual and moral compliance...NOT learning.

- ❏ Children don't learn mastery of anything there...which often graduates rebellious teens that choose self-destructive behaviors in their desire for attention and/or validation.
- ❏ There are just two people at the center of the challenging but rewarding process of intentional learning...you, and your child.

Overcoming Your Discouragement

IF we have not clearly and concretely defined the "Why" driving our intentionality, THEN one of two things almost always happens:

① **We quit and allow our child to be schooled by default, or...**

② **We simply rely on the same methods that we were schooled with and then apply this "institutionalized" approach to the education of our child.**

Overcoming Your Child's Discouragement

When students are unclear on the "Why" they will typically:

① **Comply grudgingly while internally resisting you, or...**

② **Tenaciously oppose your efforts to the very end.**

IF your child doesn't fully understand the "Why," THEN the blessing that parents are given to help their child develop virtue, character, and intellect can be squandered...*or even lost altogether.*

STEP №6: Never forget the "WHY"

The Magic Bullet?

While simply understanding the "Why" does not magically dispel the challenge of true learning, having a clarity of purpose WILL develop:

- ❏ The self-control necessary for self-education.
- ❏ The determination to work through the difficult challenges that inevitably accompany helping your child become their best.
- ❏ Mutual trust between you and your child that can be enlarged to trust God for knowing what is best…even when it is not readily apparent.

> I am, indeed, a king, because I know how to rule myself.
> —PIETRO ARETINO (1492-1556)

Moving Forward Into Victory

When you become fully aligned with your "Why" and confidently embrace the sacred responsibility of mentorship…you will stop surviving and start THRIVING.

Remember that every great endeavor… every great responsibility…also invites unwanted "guests" to the party:

- ❏ Condescension from others, and sometimes outright hostility.
- ❏ Self-doubt, insecurity, and even anxiety.
- ❏ Fears that oppose personal growth.
- ❏ Discouragement that demands resigned surrender.

However, IF your "Why" is planted deep enough—even if these unwanted guests show up—THEN you will have the strength to show them the door.

STEP №6: Never forget the "WHY"

So, what is my "Why"?

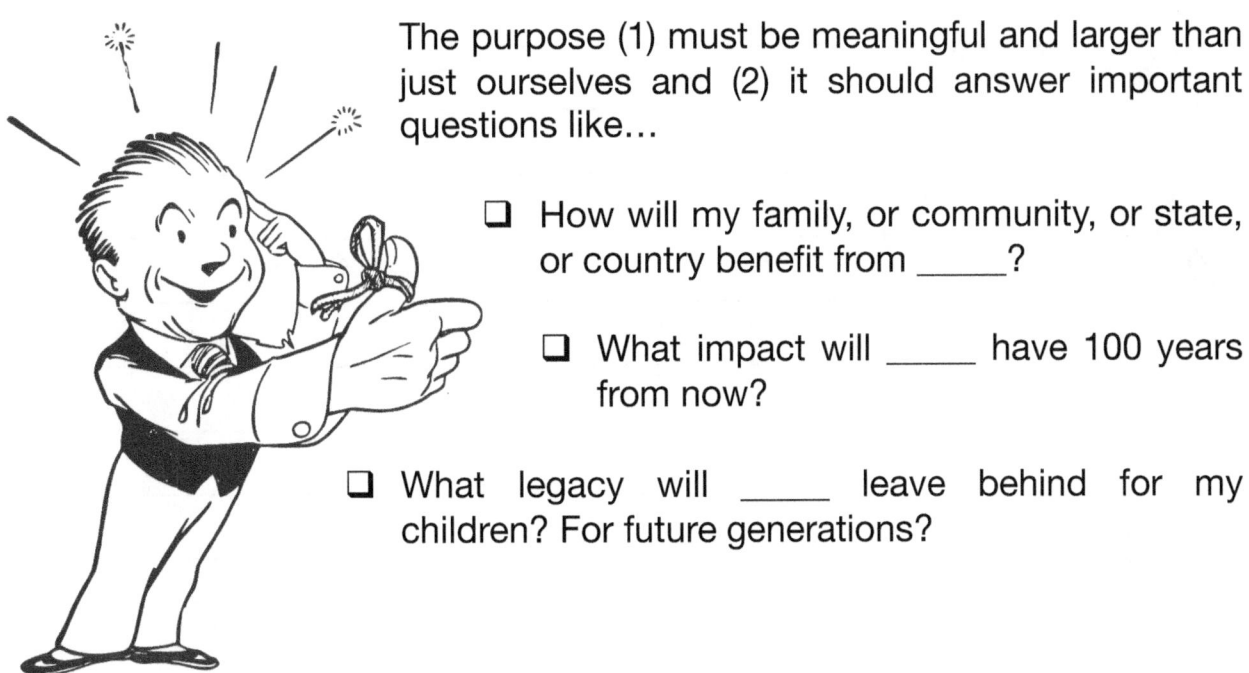

The purpose (1) must be meaningful and larger than just ourselves and (2) it should answer important questions like…

- How will my family, or community, or state, or country benefit from _____?

- What impact will _____ have 100 years from now?

- What legacy will _____ leave behind for my children? For future generations?

> **Whatever fills in these blanks must be powerful enough to greet your thoughts when you awake each morning and remain in your thoughts throughout the remainder of the day.**

- Your "Why" must be more than just a nice idea, or an inspired goal you wrote down somewhere…*it must be part of you.*

- Your "Why" must live securely within your heart and mind.

- Obstacles are inevitable…but knowing your "Why" converts them into a ladder to step up and over whatever gets in your way.

And…at least part of your "Why" is helping your children discover theirs. As Mark Twain once said, **"The two most important days of someone's life are the day they were born, and the day they find out why."**

DE-SCHOOLING IN SIX STEPS

notes

RECOMMENDED RESOURCES

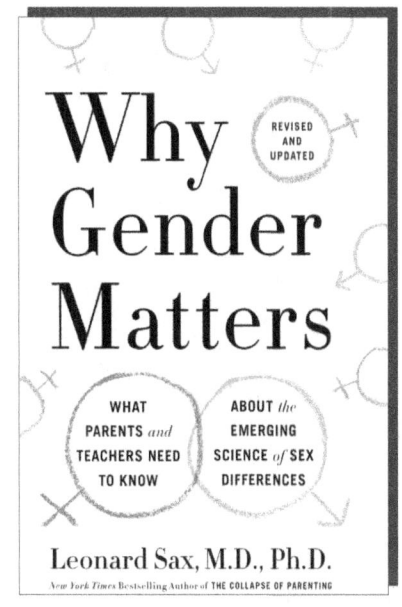

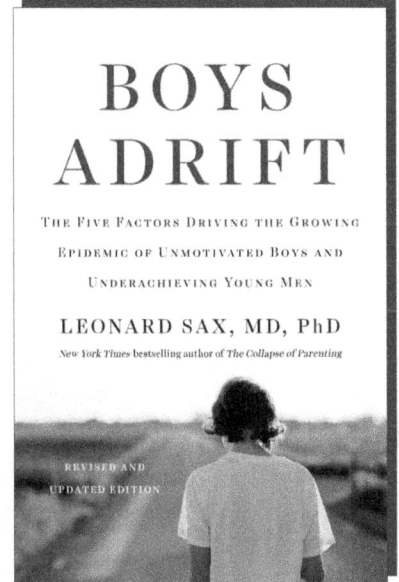

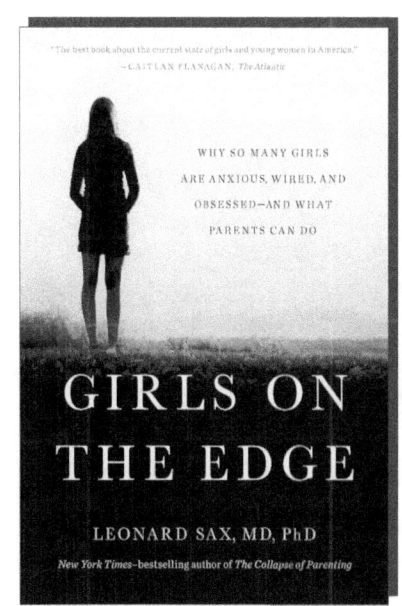

RECOMMENDED RESOURCES

THE FIVE KEYS TO SUCCESSFUL MENTORSHIP

- ❏ KEY № 1: Envision
- ❏ KEY № 2: Encourage
- ❏ KEY № 3: Empower
- ❏ KEY № 4: Extend
- ❏ KEY № 5: Emphasize

 **Enlightened. Equipped. Empowered.**

THE FIVE KEYS TO SUCCESSFUL MENTORSHIP

- ☐ KEY № 1: Envision
- ☐ KEY № 2: Encourage
- ☐ KEY № 3: Empower
- ☐ KEY № 4: Extend
- ☐ KEY № 5: Emphasize

E³ Enlightened. Equipped. Empowered.

INTRODUCTION

> It is easier to build strong boys than it is to repair broken men.
> — FREDERICK DOUGLASS (1818-1895)

How you prepare your child for life is of the utmost importance because education = discipleship. And true discipleship cannot be done by default...it requires *thoughtful, purposeful,* and *intentional* focus.

> A disciple is not above his teacher, but everyone when he is fully trained will be like his teacher.
> — PAUL OF TARSUS (5-64AD)

The development of your child's character, virtue, passion, and talent will never happen by default. It wasn't designed to.

> Your reputation is what others think of you; your character is what you truly are. Reputations can be manipulated; character can only be developed and maintained.
> — BOHDI SANDERS

Although there is certainly great value in academic study, character is the most important "subject" that your child can master.

INTRODUCTION

The seeds you sow into your children will produce fruit... but will it be the fruit you want?

YOU have already begun to answer that question...and are presently engaged in the process by...

❑ Identifying the lessons you never knew you learned in school.

❑ Discovering how to de-school yourself from those lessons.

❑ Choosing to replace those lessons...so that you can teach the right ones to your children.

Some of us are fortunate enough to look back with great fondness upon an inspiring mentor who changed the direction of our lives. Perhaps it was a teacher...a coach...a tutor...or hopefully, Mom or Dad.

But being a great mentor does not require formal accreditation...just the heart and the willingness to apply time-tested principles that guide someone into their fullest potential.

God has equipped and empowered you to be your child's greatest and most influential mentor because He believes you can do it better than anyone else.

Do you?

KEY Nº1
Envision

Before beginning to walk the path of success, you need to be clear on what that path looks like for your children in order to get there.

Success is…?

- ❏ …getting what you want, happiness is wanting what you get.
- ❏ …knowing you tried your best.
- ❏ …is not final, failure is not fatal; it is the courage to continue that counts.
- ❏ …going from failure to failure without loss of enthusiasm.
- ❏ …to laugh often and much, to win the respect of intelligent people and the affections of children, to earn the appreciation of honest critics and endure the betrayal of false friends, to appreciate beauty, to find the best in others, the leave the world a bit better, whether by a healthy child, a garden patch, or a redeemed social condition; to know that even one life has breathed easier because you have lived. This is to have succeeded.
- ❏ …helping my child to love God, others, and themselves and to embrace the purpose for which they were created.
- ❏ …someone who is an optimist in thought and a pessimist in action.

The point here is not to choose from one of the options listed above, but rather to help clarify and personalize your child's definition of success.

KEY №1: Envision

Seeing Past What You See

Always try to look past what is in front of you to see what your child can become.

Never use the "eyes" of the school system to evaluate the talents of your child:

① **Schools only focus on narrowly defined types of specific "talent" while marginalizing or ignoring the others.**

② **Since talent is seldom, if ever, conveniently found lying around in plain sight, schools never discover it; because it is usually buried and requires time, patience, and effort to uncover.**

Things To Do

❑ Watch your children closely for what sparks their interest.

❑ Take note of the things they delight in.

❑ When you discover something, help them begin drilling down into the specific components that complement their talent and/or passion.

❑ As you envision their potential, help them to reverse engineer the steps required to fulfill the destiny that they were designed for.

On To Success

❑ A wise mentor *envisions the best in their student*.

❑ Once this belief has been transferred to the child, they will become increasingly inspired to (1) emulate their mentor's virtues and (2) strive to fulfil their own potential.

KEY N°2
Encourage

Just Enough, Or Just Your Best?

Encouragement is not a reward for "just showing up" or "participating."

Our efforts have consequences (e.g., swimmer Michael Phelps, winning the 100m-butterfly by 1/100th of second at the 2008 Summer Olympic Games).

❑ What if Phelps thought excellence meant "just enough" instead of "just your best"? (There are no participant ribbons in real life).

❑ However, we must always strive to maintain a healthy balance between the desire for excellence and neurotic perfectionism. ☺

True Encouragement Builds Real Self-Esteem

Children are much brighter than we often give them credit for and will *interpret false encouragement one of two ways:*

① **Even though you know the quality of my work is terrible, you insist on telling me that it's awesome = You're a liar and cannot be trusted, or…**
② **Even though the quality of my work is terrible, you actually think that it's awesome = You're stupid and cannot be respected.**

Remind the child of the talents/skills they *already possess*.

Cast a vision for what can be achieved through **diligence** and **excellence of effort,** so they understand that:

❑ Self-esteem is based upon actual accomplishment.
❑ Self-esteem doesn't rely on artificial standards of "feel-goodism."

KEY №2: Encourage

❑ True self-satisfaction is impossible without diligence and excellence.

The Two Most Important Questions

① "Did you do your best?"

② "If you can do better…should you?"

The Most Powerful Talent

Although everyone is blessed with different gifts, *persistence and determination* are available to everyone…and are arguably *the most powerful gifts of them all*. The exercise of these gifts is entirely our choice.

Calvin Coolidge (1872-1933), the 30th President of the United States, described the power of persistence this way:

> Nothing in this world can take the place of persistence. Talent will not: nothing is more common than unsuccessful men with talent. Genius will not; unrewarded genius is almost a proverb. Education will not: the world is full of educated derelicts. Persistence and determination alone are omnipotent.
> — CALVIN COOLIDGE (1872-1933)

KEY №2: Encourage

The Apostle Paul framed the power of persistence this way, "…And don't just do the minimum that will get you by. Do your best. Work from your heart."

The Focus

Praising their *effort, not their results*, will…

- ❑ inspire the child to give their best and not, "just enough."
- ❑ reinforce excellence of effort as their primary objective.

However, just praising the student for being "smart" has one of two possible consequences:

① **The child will believe they are so "smart" that they don't have to put forth any effort (or just the bare minimum).**

② **The child will be tempted to lie, cheat, and steal to get the "score" that wins your praise and maintains their "smart" status…because they believe their best is not good enough.**

When students cheat on exams it's because our school system values grades more than students value learning.
— NEIL DEGRASSE TYSON

KEY No 3
Empower

Allowing Them To Fail

The mentor offers advice, or instruction…or guides the student to a particular expert/resource. The mentor must allow the student to make mistakes and fail, but…

- ❑ Encourage the student's recovery from those mistakes.
- ❑ Help the student to correctly interpret those mistakes.
- ❑ Remember, a mistake incorrectly interpreted can be devastating…BUT *a mistake correctly interpreted can be the path to success.*

As Sir Ken Robinson wisely noted, "If you're not prepared to be wrong, you'll never come up with anything original."

Famed inventor Thomas Edison chose to interpret his failures very differently than others did. A young reporter once boldly asked Mr. Edison if he felt like a failure and should simply give up his experiments.

Perplexed, Edison replied, "Young man, why would I feel like a failure? And why would I ever give up? I now know definitively over 9,000 ways that an electric light bulb will not work. Success is almost in my grasp."

> **To increase your rate of success, you must double your rate of failure.**
> —THOMAS EDISON (1847-1931)

KEY Nº3: Empower

In the 1990s, Nike aired a commercial featuring Michael Jordan, the greatest basketball player of his era. In the commercial, Jordan is dressed in street clothes and walks through the Chicago Bull's United Center arena into the player's dressing room while narrating the scene:

> I've missed more than 9,000 shots in my career...I've lost more than 300 games... 26 times I've been entrusted to take the game-winning shot...and missed...I've failed over and over and over in my life...and that is why...**I succeed**.

The Takeaways

Considering the legendary successes of both Edison and Jordan, it is curious that our society in general, *and the school system in particular*, views failing with such disapproval.

❑ Excellence of effort is the only measurement by which to judge results and strive for improvement.

❑ I know from personal experience that students can be freed from the burden of feeling like a failure and CAN be empowered to improve.

❑ Always praise the *effort* of the child, not how "smart" they are.

❑ Always ask your child...

- "Did you do your best?"
- "If you can do better, should you?"

KEY № 4
Extend

The Challenge Of Excellence

You never know what you are capable of until extended beyond your comfort zone.

❑ Mentors need to remind their students: *never strive to be merely average in your pursuits.*
❑ Excellence is measured solely by the *quality of effort* expended in achieving the result.

Consider UCLA's legendary basketball coach, John Wooden. During Wooden's exemplary *27-year coaching career:*

❑ …he was named National Coach-Of-The-Year six times.
❑ …he compiled an overall record of 620 wins and 147 losses.
❑ …he won 10 NCAA Division I national championship titles.
❑ …of those 10 titles, 7 were in-a-row (a "7-peat").
❑ …he recorded 4 perfect seasons of 30-0.
❑ …he once recorded an 88-game winning streak.

To put John Wooden's unrivaled success in proper perspective: the second-winningest coach of all-time, Mike Krzyzewski of Duke University, needed *41 years to win only five national titles.*

How Wooden Pushed His Players To Be Their Best

❑ He demanded that his players **extend** themselves to their personal limit.

❑ He relentlessly reminded them to focus **only** on doing their personal best, and **not** to compare themselves to others.

KEY №4: Extend

You are always playing ONLY against yourself…never your opponent.

① When confident of victory…believing that you are better than your opponent will cause you to consciously or subconsciously put forth **less than your best effort.**

② When certain of defeat…believing that your opponent is better than you will cause you to consciously or subconsciously put forth **less than your best effort.**

③ Either way, you play **less than your best**.

For Coach Wooden, all that mattered was that his players were willing to **extend** themselves as far as they could go…and not one inch less.

It is good advice…and it's kind of hard to argue with his success.

But the problem we often have with good advice is that…it's…too…simple. And of course, it is always much easier said than done. ☺

KEY № 5
Emphasize

Repetition Is The Mother Of Skill

In some ways, "Emphasize" is the most important of the five keys because without it, you cannot experience the full benefit of the other four.

❑ The student must *review, repeat, drill, practice,* to master something.

❑ And mastery never truly ends.

Impatience Is Your Enemy

❑ Unfortunately, we live in a "I want it yesterday" culture that dismisses the value of consistent practice over time.

❑ Avoid falling prey to New Year's Resolution Syndrome…instead, resolve to "give up on giving up" *and just keep going.*

KEY №5: Emphasize

At The End Of The Day

Knowledge is NOT power...*knowledge APPLIED is power.*

① **Envision**. Watch for what sparks your child's interest and help them drill down into those specific areas that complement their talents and passion. Give them a vision for what they could be.

② **Encourage**. Use appropriate praise for your child's *efforts not the outcome* to develop a "just your best" attitude instead of a "just enough" attitude. But...be careful to maintain an appropriate balance so that the desire for excellence doesn't become distorted into neurotic perfectionism.

③ **Empower**. Offer your child advice, instruction, or recommend a suitable expert or resource. Assuming that your child is *doing their best*, give them room to fail and help them correctly interpret their mistakes.

④ **Extend**. Encourage your child to extend themselves by attempting new challenges, helping them correctly interpret mistakes, and reminding them not to compare themselves to others. *Just. Do. Your. Best. Period.*

⑤ **Emphasize**. Consistently review and practice the previous four keys. *The power of repetition builds mastery...and mastery builds confidence...and confidence produces results.*

THE FIVE KEYS...

notes

RECOMMENDED RESOURCES

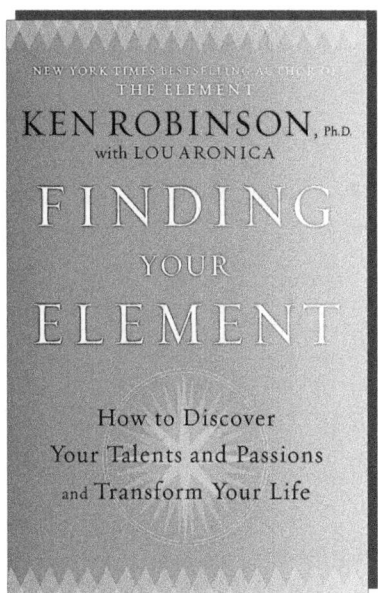

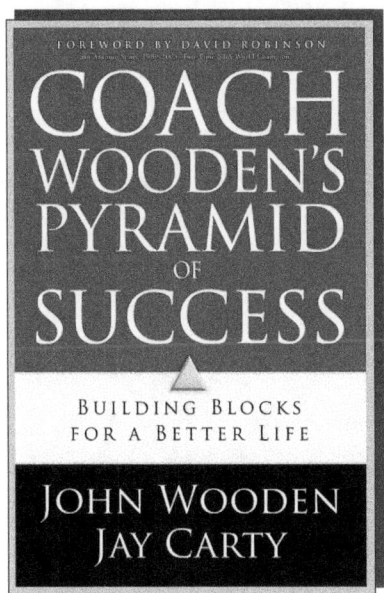

RECOMMENDED RESOURCES

a brief history

Schooling VS. EDUCATION

a brief history

SCHOOLING VS. EDUCATION: A brief history

Introduction

Remember that knowledge is NOT power...*knowledge APPLIED is power.*

This is an opportunity to apply the ideas that you have just learned, and to embrace the journey of intentional parenting.

As a quick review:

- *The two greatest fears of every parent are actually the two greatest strengths of every parent.*
- *Those two fears are largely the product of the seven lessons we never knew we learned in school.*
- *Once identified, we can begin de-schooling our minds from those seven lessons in six simple (but not easy) steps.*
- *As we continue the process of de-schooling, it is crucial that we apply the five keys of mentorship to help our children discover their highest potential.*

Once we embrace this new paradigm concerning how to prepare our kids for life, the difference between being educated and being schooled becomes much clearer.

Thus, the new paradigm of education = to engage a child in each of the five dimensions of development (spiritual, emotional, mental, social, physical) in order to fully prepare them for life as the best version of themselves.

With this in mind, we need to briefly re-examine how true education happens.

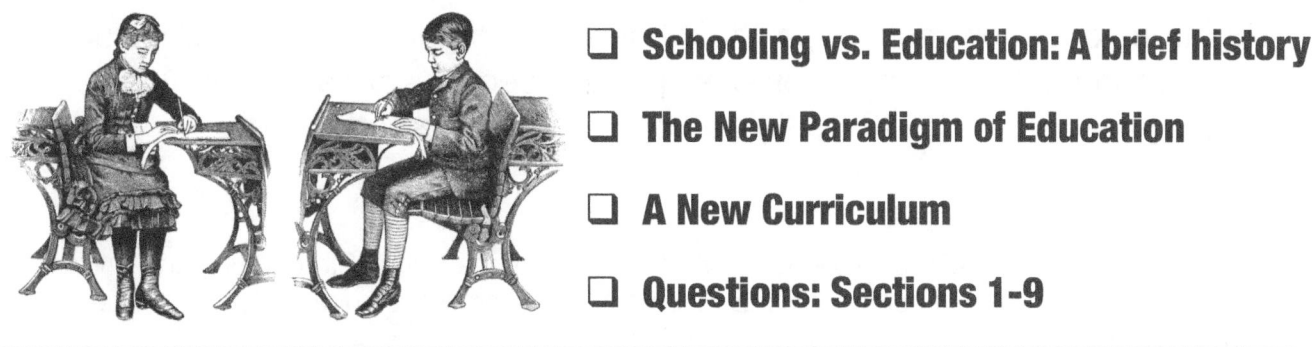

- Schooling vs. Education: A brief history
- The New Paradigm of Education
- A New Curriculum
- Questions: Sections 1-9

SCHOOLING VS. EDUCATION: A brief history

The "Founding Fathers" Of Modern Schooling

The nature and purpose of our modern school system can only be understood through the ideology of its "founding fathers" (e.g., Horace Mann, John Dewey, G. Stanley Hall, Edward Thorndike, Ellwood Cubberly, etc.). However, these men were not the exclusive creators of this system.

Their efforts were supported by the leaders of America's industrialist class...men like Andrew Carnegie (steel); John D. Rockefeller (oil); Henry Ford (automobile+assembly line); J. P. Morgan (banking); and Frederick W. Taylor[1] (the brilliant efficiency expert).

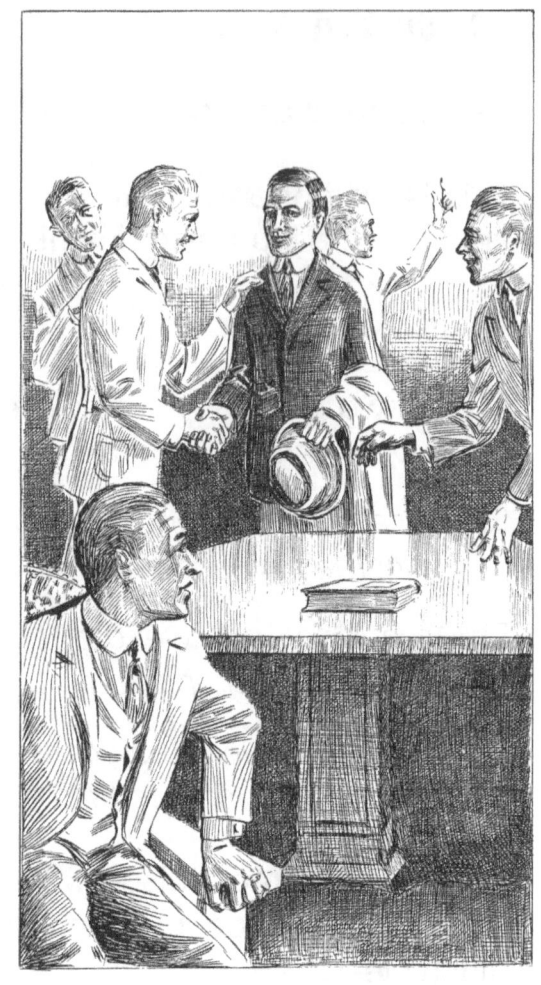

However, while these educators and industrialists are rightly considered the co-creators of modern schooling, they did not wield the greatest influence. That dubious distinction goes to, "quiet men in grey suits in a suburb of New York City called Princeton, New Jersey."

These men from Princeton developed and promoted standardized testing (e.g., IQ, PSAT, SAT, ACT, AP, GRE, etc.) in an effort to place children into more easily managed categories. The tests they created (and this point cannot be emphasized enough) *completely redefined what it means to learn.*

This transformation resulted in the wholesale reorganization of curriculum to accommodate these tests. A process popularized by educational psychologist Dr. Benjamin Bloom (1913-1999) as, "outcomes-based education."

---

[1] Taylor inspired America's "social efficiency" movement of the early 20th century, and provided the Soviet Union, fascist Italy, and Nazi Germany with the infrastructure for their operating philosophies.

SCHOOLING VS. EDUCATION: A brief history

The Fourth Purpose

Together, these men—and the organizations they created—imagined a grand future based upon their ideas. Although the utopia they envisioned was hardly the product of conspiracy, these various individuals and groups collectively pressed toward a common goal for schooling, a "Fourth Purpose" if you will.

Of course, to suggest that modern compulsory schooling represents a "Fourth Purpose" implies there were three others that preceded it.

The traditional purpose of education in America (from pre-Revolutionary War to c. 1890) generally advanced three primary goals:

1. **To make virtuous people.**

2. **To make good colonists/citizens.**

3. **To make each student discover their particular talents, and to develop those talents to the fullest extent possible.**

However, the new mass schooling, which evolved slowly but continuously after 1890, ominously advanced this "fourth" purpose instead.

In fact, the fourth purpose steadily pushed the traditional three to the margins of education until schooling in America more closely resembled that of Germany (where it had been designed to produce servants of corporate and political interests).

The process of institutionalizing this form of intellectual servitude can be best understood as a *conditioning mechanism for training predictable thinking, habits, and attitudes.*

Consequently, students were literally trained in self-limiting thoughts, habits, and attitudes! Moreover, since both teachers and principals were "scientifically certified" in teacher's colleges, they remained largely unaware of the invisible curriculum they were actually indoctrinating their students into.

SCHOOLING VS. EDUCATION: A brief history

The secret of commerce—that *children drive purchases*—meant that schools had to become psychological laboratories where *training in consumerism was the central, or "Fourth Purpose."*

"Corporate" Schooling

The fourth purpose was based on two core principles:

① Bored people are the best consumers. Therefore, school had to become a boring place that conditioned children to "normalize" and endure boredom.

② Childish people are the easiest consumers to exploit. Therefore, the manufacturing of childishness—extended as far into adulthood as possible—became the first priority of schooling.

Naturally, teachers and administrators weren't informed of these operating principles; they didn't need to be. If they didn't follow the directives passed down from increasingly centralized school bureaucracies, they didn't last long.

Educrats gradually reorganized schools to meet the critical need of corporate interests for standardized customers and employees. Thus, they further reduced students into predictable "mathematical formulas." These "formulas" could then be used to improve efficiency in business and government by manufacturing "redesigned" human beings that met these simplified specifications.

SCHOOLING VS. EDUCATION: A brief history

The Edutocracy's Growing Influence

Consequently, from the 1890's onward, each passing decade saw the edutocracy expand its influence and gradually open more school spaces to the interests of commercialization.

Of course, these processes experienced uneven expansion. Some localities resisted more than others, and some decades advanced the plan further than others. But the periods of favorable advancement almost always coincided with the aftermath of national emergencies: World War I, the Great Depression, World War II, the Sputnik crisis, etc. In less turbulent times, the plan lost momentum, or was even forced to retreat.

However, even in those moments of greatest resistance, the institutions controlling the fourth purpose (e.g., large corporations, hallowed universities, government bureaus with vast powers to reward or punish, and corporate journalism) became *increasingly centralized into fewer and fewer hands* throughout the 20th and 21st centuries.

Perhaps even more importantly, these institutions now possessed considerable resources to simply wear down and outwait any opposition.

After all, what better way to convince children to abandon trust in both their peers and themselves, than to create an atmosphere of constant low-level stress (e.g., grades, class ranking, behavior compliance, etc.) in which relief was *only available by appealing to authority*? [And often, not even then!]

The power sought by the "Founding Fathers" of modern schooling was nothing less than the complete control of young minds...and therefore, the future (*all for the benefit of society of course*).

SCHOOLING VS. EDUCATION: A brief history

"Unsafe" Schooling

Beginning in 1890, wherever mass schooling was introduced (1) gradually became "de-personalized" (2) and increasingly viewed children as "human resources." Human resource children are molded and shaped for something called "The Workplace," even though for most of U.S. history, American children were raised with the expectation of creating their own workplaces.

However, in this new paradigm, most Americans were trained for employment in large corporations or government bureaucracies…if they worked at all.

This transformation of the American dream produced some rather unpleasant byproducts. Since systematized forms of employment demand that employees become highly specialized in *specific* functions of production…then it follows that *incomplete people make the best corporate and government employees*.

Earlier Americans like James Madison and Thomas Jefferson were keenly aware of this paradox…which, in modern times, has been largely forgotten at best, or deliberately ignored at worst.

Consequently, one of the *most important tasks of compulsory government schooling is* the mass production of standardized students who have been trained to think and behave predictably in order to achieve future social efficiency.

Not only was this new type of institution intellectually and emotionally unsafe, but it also became physically unsafe as well (e.g., school violence, bullying, etc.).

Ironically, Horace Mann sold compulsory schooling to industrialists of the mid-19th century as the best "police" to create "moral" children.

SCHOOLING VS. EDUCATION: A brief history

School As A Prison Of Pointless Pressure

As the 20th century progressed—particularly after World War II—schools evolved into behavioral training centers and experimental laboratories that served the joint interests of corporations and government. The original model for this development had been Prussian Germany, but by then, few remembered.

School became the equivalent of serving jail-time—something to escape if you could. Conditions inside these prisons of pointless pressure were further worsened by the omnipresent "standardized" exams (which numerous studies have confirmed as a useless metric of learning).

But to truly comprehend just *how* useless these learning metrics are, consider the field of science. And perhaps, the clearest illustration of this is that standardized tests are incapable of identifying either good or bad scientists.

How else to explain the fact that the two American scientists principally involved in the Human Genome Project have such…um…"eclectic scholarly backgrounds"?

SCHOOLING VS. EDUCATION: A brief history

- ❑ Francis S. Collins, physician-geneticist, noted for his discoveries of disease genes and his oversight on the Human Genome Project (HGP), was homeschooled, never followed any type of formal curriculum, and is a born-again Christian.

- ❑ Craig Venter, biologist and entrepreneur, was a surf bum who nearly flunked out of high school, enlisted in the U.S. Army instead of attending college, and was shipped off to Vietnam. He is widely acclaimed as one of the first scientists to sequence the human genome and to create the first cell with a synthetic genome and is an atheist.

School As A Prison Of Confused Boredom

As you'll discover when you read John Taylor Gatto's, *The Underground History of American Education*, the true purpose of modern schooling—to serve the interests of business and government—could only be achieved by efficiently isolating children from the real world…led by adults who were themselves isolated from the real world…and with everyone in the system isolated from one another.

When this process of systematized isolation was complete, everyone could be more easily placed into an artificial bubble where the basic training in confused boredom and enforced childishness could begin.

As previously noted, such training is absolutely necessary to produce predictable consumers and dependent citizens who have been conditioned to rely upon an "authority" (i.e., expert) to tell them what to do (and what to think)…whether that "authority" is a teacher, a celebrity, a journalist, a television news personality, an advertising executive, or a politician.

After all, it is far easier for educrats to brainwash boys and girls, than it is for them to conquer the minds of independent men and women.

the NEW PARADIGM of Education

the NEW PARADIGM of Education

THE NEW PARADIGM OF EDUCATION

How Does It All Work?

Of course, it's one thing to prescribe 'intentionality' as the antidote to the school system's standardized poison of mediocrity, but quite another to effect the cure.

It bears repeating that a clear contrast must be drawn between the thinking and behaviors advocated by the compulsory school system, and what is meant by intentional education. That clarity becomes even more evident by carefully observing what students **do** in the classroom.

For example:

…John Dewey (1859-1952) would likely argue that what students **do** in a classroom is what they learn.

…Marshall McLuhan (1911-1980) would probably add that what they **learn to do** is the classroom's message.

So, we return to the original question: what is it that students actually **do** in the classroom?

- ❑ They are required to sit and listen attentively to the teacher.
- ❑ They are required to unquestioningly believe what their teachers/textbooks say is true (or at least pretend to when taking standardized tests).
- ❑ They are required to *regurgitate whatever selection of "facts" that the teacher/state has deemed most important.*

BUT they are seldom, IF EVER, required to observe, formulate definitions, or perform any intellectual activity beyond correctly repeating what a teacher/textbook has told them to be true.

Although they are rarely permitted to ask meaningful questions, they are relentlessly encouraged to ask about *administrative and technical details*.

Details like…

THE NEW PARADIGM OF EDUCATION

- "When is the assignment due?"
- "How long should the paper be?"
- "Does spelling and grammar count?"
- "What if we turn it in late?"
- "How much does this count toward my final grade?"

It is virtually unheard of for students to be *meaningfully involved* in determining which problems or ideas are worth studying, or what procedures of inquiry should be used to study those ideas.

The Way It Works In The Classroom

If you pay close attention to the kinds of questions that teachers typically ask in the classroom, you will discover that they almost always fall into the category of "deductive inquiry." Just in case you don't have your *Dictionary of Pretentious Words That Hide What's Actually Being Said* handy…these are also called, "Guess what I'm thinking" questions. It's really a Trivia Game pretending to be education.

Consequently, the most "successful" students are those who most accurately and consistently regurgitate whatever the teacher/textbook has told them is "true."

To be perfectly blunt, the school system's curriculum is really a strategy of distraction…and is largely designed to **prevent** students from experiencing a meaningful discovery of themselves, or their environment. In fact, students are **actively prevented** from exploring the content of the real world outside the artificial confinement of school.

It should be noted that the primary difference between the "advantaged" and "disadvantaged" student is that the former has an economic stake in following the curriculum that the latter does not. Put another way, the curriculum's only value for the "advantaged" student is that doing what he/she is told produces a tangible payoff (e.g., college).

However, if every college professor in America rejected the status quo and adopted a neo-Socratic pedagogy, it would instantly eliminate the need for a methods course. Because **every** course would be a methods of learning course…and, by default, involve methods of teaching.

For example, a literature course would be a course in the process of learning how to read the classics. A history course would be a course in the process of learning how to study history. And so on.

Unfortunately, this is the unlikeliest of all possible outcomes, since college professors are far more obsessed with the Trivia game than any other member of the educational hierarchy. Moreover, if a methods course was ever redesigned to model real learning environments, it would likely fan the flames of an educational revolution.

How Should It All Work?

Bear in mind that this transformation will not happen until the system absorbs a critical mass of young teachers who sufficiently despise the crippling educational environments they are employed to supervise. The moment this tipping point is reached, their subversion would almost certainly escalate into a "revolution" that [ideally] should advance the following steps:

1. Eliminate all conventional / standardized "tests" and "testing."
2. Eliminate all "courses."
3. Eliminate all "requirements."
4. Eliminate all full-time "administrators" and "administrations."
5. Eliminate any restriction that confines learners to sitting inside boxes inside of boxes.

It is hardly coincidental that the five conditions requiring elimination are also the five biggest obstacles to actual learning.

Children have subsequently become trapped in a school system that expends almost all its energies and resources to preserve its own structures, patterns, and procedures (while offering virtually no educational value).

THE NEW PARADIGM OF EDUCATION

In fact, this same system has comprehensively failed to produce the results that supposedly justified its existence in the first place.

Without a trace of shame, the edutocracy loudly proclaims the purpose of schooling is to train students to be "fully functioning, self-renewing citizens of democracy." Seriously? So, basically, they are saying that...the artificial supports propping up the ever-increasing socio-economic cost of a system that sentences our youth to 13 years of intellectual servitude in a totalitarian environment...*is* "worth it?" Based upon what results?

Instead...imagine for a moment how implementing just these five suggestions (hat tip to Neil Postman) could create an environment that prepares individuals to explore and step into their fullest potential.

1. Eliminate all conventional/standardized testing... The moment that standardized tests are used to rank, categorize, or otherwise evaluate a student...everything changes. The entire purpose of schooling immediately shifts from the training of the intellect, to the spoon-feeding of predigested thoughts to ensure the successful regurgitation of arbitrarily assigned "sets of data" (i.e., tests).

2. Eliminate all courses... The value of a "course" is entirely dependent upon conventional/standardized testing. A "course" generally consists of a series of scripted reviews in preparation for the great Trivia contest (i.e., test). It's really nothing more than a highly structured and predictable quiz show. And it only works IF the contestants value the "prize."

The prize, of course, is a "good grade" that entitles the participant to advance to the next round of the Trivia game (i.e., college). Keep in mind, however, that this entire process discourages meaningful mental, emotional, and social engagement.

3. Eliminate all "requirements"... Conventional "requirements" are merely systems designed to limit the mental and emotional growth of students in order to "keep them in line." This is best accomplished by changing the focus of attention from the **learner** (cf. Goodwin Watson) to the **"course."** In a stunning violation of nearly every known aspect of how real learning occurs, the "requirements" form the foundation for an elaborate system of punishments

THE NEW PARADIGM OF EDUCATION

that creates a threatening atmosphere that stifles positive learning.

Consequently, the "requirements" *force both the teacher and the administrator* to assume the role of an authoritarian figure whose primary task is to enforce the requirements, instead of helping the learner to learn. Bottom line: the system's entire authority structure hinges upon meeting the "requirements."

4. Eliminate all full-time "administrators" and "administrations"... Public school administrators owe their positions to the self-serving nature of an edutocracy that has long-since forgotten its reason for existence.

Moreover, the attention of these administrators (at least during school hours) is almost exclusively preoccupied with addressing various problems created by the "requirements." Therefore, they seldom see, hear, or engage the people that the system supposedly serves — the students.

The concept that schools should consist of methods specifically designed to help learners learn would offend most administrators who would likely dismiss such ideas as absurd and "impractical." After all, their job is simply to enforce the "requirements" and "follow orders" as directed by the edutocracy.

However, at the risk of abusing a well-worn cliché...it's worth remembering that Eichmann[2] and Goebbels[3] were just "administrators" who merely enforced "requirements" and "followed orders."

Even the notion of employing "full-time administrators" ranks among the very worst of the edutocracy's endlessly horrible ideas...especially since it usurps the true purpose of education. (Or, at least it would, if schools operated according to the pedagogical ideals to which they pay lip service).

So...this begs the question: "What should we replace administrators with"?

---

[2] Adolf Eichmann served as a Nazi SS-lieutenant colonel and was responsible for the logistical facilitation and management of the mass deportation of Jews to ghettos and extermination camps in Eastern Europe during World War II.

[3] Joseph Goebbels was a Nazi politician and served as Hitler's Reich Minister of Propaganda. He was also a fanatical advocate for the complete extermination of the Jews in the Holocaust.

THE NEW PARADIGM OF EDUCATION

Three words. Head. Of. School. The ONLY way forward is to restore a classical model of education in which a Head of School oversees the Head of Grammar (grades K-6), Head of Logic (grades 7-8), and Head of Rhetoric (grades 9-12).

We could go into much greater detail here, but basically, it would look something like this...

HEAD OF SCHOOL: Visionary Leadership And Institutional Integrity

The Head of School oversees the entire institution, ensuring that the mission of the classical model—developing students in wisdom, virtue, and eloquence—is faithfully implemented. *They collaborate with...*

- *Teachers* by providing direction, encouragement, and professional development, and ensuring pedagogical consistency while allowing for their unique talents to inspire their students.

- *Parents* by engaging them in the classical model and fostering a culture of partnership in their child's education. Parents are primary...but not solitary.

- *Students* by cultivating an environment where they see leadership modeled with wisdom and integrity.

HEAD OF GRAMMAR: Laying The Foundation For Knowledge

The Head of Grammar oversees instruction in the grammar stage (grades K-6), ensuring that students develop a strong foundation in memorization, rules of grammar, phonics, Latin, arithmetic, and biblical studies. *They collaborate with...*

- *Teachers* by supporting their efforts to implement engaging, memory-based teaching methods.

- *Parents* by facilitating the reinforcement of memory work at home and helping develop a love of learning.

- *Students* by creating a structured, joyful learning experience that builds confidence in acquiring knowledge.

THE NEW PARADIGM OF EDUCATION

HEAD OF LOGIC: Training In Sound Reasoning

The Head of Logic oversees instruction in the logic stage (grades 7-8), ensuring that students learn how to analyze arguments, detect fallacies, and develop reasoned conclusions. *They collaborate with...*

- *Teachers* by supporting their implementation of effective Socratic discussion and dialectical teaching methods.

- *Parents* by encouraging curiosity and respectful debate at home.

- *Students* by equipping them to think critically and articulate their thoughts coherently.

HEAD OF RHETORIC: Cultivating Articulate And Virtuous Communicators

The Head of Rhetoric oversees instruction in the rhetoric stage (grades 9-12), helping students to synthesize their thinking and refine their ability to persuasively express ideas in speech and writing. *They collaborate with...*

- *Teachers* to mentor students in classical rhetoric, debate, and thesis development.

- *Parents* to foster engagement with students in meaningful discourse outside of the classroom.

- *Students* to inspire them to become articulate, persuasive, and wise communicators.

Although the classical model operates within defined spheres of educational authority, it strongly encourages continuous collaboration between the leadership, faculty, parents, and students by:

- Ensuring clear transitions between the three stages of learning to create a seamless educational experience.

- Providing specialized leadership that allows for focused mentorship and professional development.

THE NEW PARADIGM OF EDUCATION

- Developing a culture of partnership, where parents are actively involved, and teachers are equipped with clear guidance.

- Equipping students holistically, preparing them to learn well (Grammar), think well (Logic), and speak well (Rhetoric).

By aligning its structure with the trivium, a classical school cultivates academic rigor, character development, and intellectual formation, ensuring that each student is prepared for lifelong learning and virtuous leadership.

non scholæ sed vitæ discimus
[we do not learn for school, but for life]

EX LIBRIS

THE NEW PARADIGM OF EDUCATION

It is difficult to imagine the magnitude of lost learning suffered by generations of students who continue to graduate from public schools without ever taking their rightful place as co-developers of the operational policies, procedures, and curricula that guide the process of self-directed learning.

The "efficiency" of this form of academic totalitarianism is deceptively appealing, BUT the so-called "inefficiency" of democracy remains the *best hope* for improving the future of our children. Schools would do well to acknowledge this—or at least act as though it were true.

5. Eliminate the "boxes" of education... It is an entirely avoidable tragedy that the classroom has become the last place a student can expect to learn anything important concerning the realities they experience in the world while engaging in the daily pursuit of "life, liberty, and happiness."

For instance, what if schools required students to learn the concepts and skills relevant to the cyber-nuclear-space age? It's rather unlikely they would spend much time sitting inside small boxes inside of larger boxes while playing with the high-tech, cutting-edge technology developed to mass-market the Trivia contest of standardized testing.

Moreover, it seems fair to suggest that virtually every piece of knowledge worth knowing...can be acquired somewhere else other than public school.

The Pitfalls Of Modern Schooling

In fact, modern developments in processing electronic information have made schooling in its present form *unnecessary at best*, and *completely irrelevant at worst*.

In sharp contrast, the purpose of "intentional education" is to develop students whose ability to learn-how-to-learn enables them to adapt and thrive in a constantly changing environment.

To date, **none** of the new "educational technology" can honestly claim that as its purpose.

THE NEW PARADIGM OF EDUCATION

As Spanish philosopher George Santayana (1863-1952) wisely noted: "Fanaticism consists of redoubling your efforts after having forgotten one's aim."

The truth is, all of the "new developments" in "educational technology" are really nothing more than updated programs attempting to repackage the "requirements" of the Trivia game.

The Three Ideas We Must Learn And Apply

To be fully intentional concerning our educational choices, there are three essential ideas that must be understood to avoid the pitfalls of modern schooling:

1. Literacy.
2. Judgments.
3. Survival.

Idea No. 1: Literacy

If we imagine the learning mediums in which we have been indoctrinated into as a "prison," then it follows that securing our freedom is our only objective. But in order to win our freedom, we need to educate ourselves concerning its processes (i.e., *what the medium does and how the medium works*).

Moreover, whenever we choose to remain imprisoned by the processes of any learning medium, we are choosing to live at the mercy of those who hold the "keys."

It is for this reason that these new "learning mediums" are among the most important "subjects" to be studied. However, in order to become literate in their use, we must change the way in which they are learned. In fact, they must be studied *as something that forms and changes our perceptions.*

Indeed, for any "subject" or "discipline" to be *truly understood*, it must be studied in this way.

THE NEW PARADIGM OF EDUCATION

Idea No. 2: Judgments

We also need to become more conscious concerning the way in which we form judgments about someone, or something. This does not mean we should abandon sensible discernment. However, the moment we judge someone, or something, we almost always stop *thinking* about them, or it.

Consequently, much of our behavior is really just a response to our judgments, rather than to the object that is being judged. This is why it is crucial to understand that people and things are a "process"...until judgments convert them into fixed categories. Then, once they have been converted into a category, they often become self-fulfilling labels.

For example, in a student's early years they are judged to be "dumb" and a "nonreader." This sets into motion a series of teacher/student interactions that reinforce the initial judgment until it becomes self-fulfilling. Therefore, suspending or delaying judgements about our children is an important step towards helping them become the best version of themselves.

There is no time like the present to practice suspending judgement! ☺

Idea No. 3: Survival

Historically, most "educational" systems—*from training patterns in "primitive" tribal societies to schooling in technological societies*—exclusively promote the preservation of old ideas, concepts, attitudes, skills, and perceptions. America's public-school system is no different. In fact, its primary purpose is to ensure its own survival by training us to think of education in a very specifically defined way.

This function is largely the result of the reinforced belief that maintaining standardized, predictable thought and behavior are necessary for stability. Moreover, since survival in a stable environment depends almost entirely upon retaining successful strategies from the past...it can be confidently stated that the preservation and transmission of these strategies is the primary mission of schooling, **not learning.**

THE NEW PARADIGM OF EDUCATION

However, a paradox emerges whenever *change—not stability—*becomes the primary focus. That is because survival in a rapidly changing environment depends almost entirely upon identifying which of the old ideas/skills apply to the new threats to survival...and which ones do not.

Consequently, a new educational task becomes critical:

- Convince the student to "unlearn" (or forget) any irrelevant concepts as a condition of learning. (In other words, "selective forgetting" is a necessity for survival in such a system).

Perhaps the learning goals of **intentional education** can be best described as:

- ...becoming "literate" in various mediums of learning.
- ...becoming free from restrictive judgements and the prison of self-fulfilling labels.
- ...becoming the best version of oneself through cultivating a love of learning that develops the ability to "learn-how-to-learn."

Conclusion

Ultimately, intentionality develops:

- Students who have learned to self-educate and internalize different concepts.
  - Students who are virtuous, actively inquisitive, flexible, creative, innovative, and compassionate.
  - Students who can face uncertainty and ambiguity without disorientation.
  - Students who are resilient in the face of obstacles and setbacks.
- Students who can formulate viable new ideas and methods to adapt to environmental changes that threaten both individual and collective survival.

The movement to choose intentionality has begun, and *if you don't think for yourself...someone else will always be more than happy to think for you!*

THE NEW PARADIGM OF EDUCATION

Every parent's mission is to help their children become the best version of themselves by fully engaging in the five dimensions of development. Though the effort will not end with us, it must start somewhere…one child at a time.

"Children are our greatest treasure. They are our future."
— Nelson Mandela

THE NEW PARADIGM OF EDUCATION

A NEW CURRICULUM

A NEW CURRICULUM

A NEW CURRICULUM

Just Imagine

Suppose for a moment, that every syllabus, curricula, and textbook in the entire public-school system vanished overnight. Imagine that every standardized test—city, state, and national—simply disappeared. In this hypothetical scenario, all the "educational" material that has been the greatest obstacle to real education…has simply evaporated into smoke.

Now, suppose you decided to transform this "catastrophe" into an opportunity to reconstruct the educational system from the ground up. What would you do?

SOCRATES
(470–399 BC)

I am going to suggest that the entire "curriculum" should consist of questions. A form of "neo-Socratic" dialogue if you will.

- ❏ The questions should be based solely upon whether the mentor (and the student) found the questions *worth the time and effort* required to find the answers.

- ❏ Ideally, the questions should inspire the student to…

  - develop a better understanding of God, themselves, others, and how life works and…

- internalize concepts that (1) empower them to discover the best version of themselves, (2) equip them to learn-how-to-learn, and (3) enable them to thrive in a rapidly changing world.

As the French Enlightenment philosopher Voltaire (1694-1778) sagely advised, **"Judge a man by his questions rather than by his answers."**

So what questions are worth asking?

First, we need to look at how questions are formed before evaluating which ones deserve to be answered:

A NEW CURRICULUM

1. When given the freedom to ask questions, children often challenge the thinking of adults.

2. If carefully listened to, questions will often present themselves even when children aren't actually the ones asking the questions.

3. Children often make declarative statements about things in an attempt to elicit an informative response. But irrespective of the reason, a simple translation of their declarative statements often reveals a broad variety of deeply felt questions.

4. Sometimes, children are simply mirroring what they learned from adults: (i.e., it is "better" to pretend that you know than to admit that you don't). A timeless adage describing this process states: "Children enter school as question marks and leave as periods."

5. In other instances, there are certain questions that children literally do not know how to ask.

When considered from the child's point of view, there can be little doubt that these questions are far more meaningful than the spoon-fed regurgitations of pre-selected ideas offered by standardized tests and curricula.

Contrary to conventional school practices, true education enables the mentor to *assess what the student already knows* so that the student can be trained in the arts of testing, verifying, reordering, reclassifying, modifying, and synthesizing information.

Consequently, when a student achieves a level of mastery in these arts, they will have acquired the ability to self-educate and no endeavor will be beyond their grasp.

Throughout this process, the student is not merely a passive "recipient" but instead becomes an active producer of knowledge. The word "educate" is closely related to the word "educe." In the classic pedagogical use of the term, it described a mentor drawing out the potential or talent from their student.

A NEW CURRICULUM

Yet, contrary to one of the most common educational myths, *we can only learn in relation to what we already know.*

This means that limited learning = limited capacity for learning. Just this idea alone demands a major revision of the teaching philosophies that presently shape school policies and procedures.

Moreover, this point is so important that it's worth repeating: these questions are **not** intended as a "catechism" for intentional education. I am merely suggesting that these questions are *among those worth asking.* In fact, you might even prefer your own questions to those listed in this workbook.

Intentionality is not diminished by the committed imaginations of those who seek to participate in the process…rather, it is improved by it.

However, a word of caution. As you evaluate these questions—as well as your own—bear in mind that certain **principles** should be observed. Unsurprisingly, these principles are also best expressed as questions:

❑ Will your questions increase the both the learner's **desire** and **capacity** to learn? Will they inspire a **love** of learning? Will they build the learner's **confidence** in their ability to learn?

❑ In order to find answers, will the learner be required to make inquiries? (i.e., ask additional questions, clarify terms, make observations, classify data, etc.)?

❑ Does each question allow for alternative answers (which also implies alternative methods of inquiry)?

❑ Does the process of answering the questions consider the **uniqueness** of the learner? Will the answers facilitate the learner's ability to identify and understand universal ideas concerning their view of God, themselves, others, and how life works? (All of which enhances their ability to draw closer to others).

I strongly encourage you to set aside some time to thoughtfully reflect on the

A NEW CURRICULUM

following questions—and any additional ones they may inspire. They were written to purposely avoid reactive responses, so please don't just answer, "Yes" or "No."

The easiest thing in the world is to write down whatever seems like the "right" answer and then quickly move on to the next question. However, since this is NOT a timed, standardized test, please carefully consider your responses (which can be re-asked and can also change over time).

Lastly, these questions do not come with an answer key...because there isn't one. (This is not to suggest that we can arbitrarily invent our own reality in which whatever we want to be true, is true). ☺

However, there are no "easy" answers to these questions, and they all require thoughtful deliberation...so please don't short-change yourself by blowing through them.

The purpose here is not to establish a "question template" or a "question curriculum", nor is it to suggest that these are the only questions that should be asked. Rather, it is an attempt to offer some examples of questions that are worth asking in the hopes that they will inspire your own. The following selection of questions were adapted from Neil Postman and various other sources.

He who has a why to live for can bear almost any how.

— FRIEDRICH NIETZSCHE

QUESTIONS: Section 1

QUESTIONS: Section 1

1. What do you worry most about?

QUESTIONS: Section 1

2. What are the causes of your worries?

QUESTIONS: Section 1

3. Can any of your worries be eliminated? If so, how?

QUESTIONS: Section 1

4. Which of these worries should be addressed first? How do you decide?

QUESTIONS: Section 1

5. Are there other people with the same worries? How do you know? How can you find out?

Judge a man by his questions rather than by his answers.

— M. DE VOLTAIRE

QUESTIONS: Section 2

QUESTIONS: Section 2

1. What bothers you most about adults? Why?

QUESTIONS: Section 2

2. Someday, you will be an adult yourself, so how do you want to be similar and/or different from the adults you know?

QUESTIONS: Section 2

3. What actions can you take to become similar? To become different? What sources will you rely upon to decide what actions to take?

If they can get you asking the wrong questions, they don't have to worry about answers.

— THOMAS PYNCHON

QUESTIONS: Section 3

QUESTIONS: Section 3

1. What, if anything, is worth dying for?

QUESTIONS: Section 3

2. How did you come to believe this?

QUESTIONS: Section 3

3. What seems worth living for?

QUESTIONS: Section 3

4. How did you come to believe this?

QUESTIONS: Section 3

5. What makes life meaningful?

Most misunderstandings in the world could be avoided if people would simply take the time to ask, 'What else could this mean?'

— SHANNON L. ALDER

QUESTIONS: Section 4

QUESTIONS: Section 4

1. At this present moment, what would you most like to be? To be able to do? Why?

QUESTIONS: Section 4

2. What would you have to know/learn to be able to do it?

QUESTIONS: Section 4

3. What or who would be the best source to learn this from?

Have patience with everything that remains unsolved in your heart. Try to love the questions themselves, like locked rooms and like books written in a foreign language. Do not now look for the answers. They cannot now be given to you because you could not live them. It is a question of experiencing everything. At present you need to live the question. Perhaps you will gradually, without even noticing it, find yourself experiencing the answer, some distant day.

—RAINER MARIA RILKE

QUESTIONS: Section 5

QUESTIONS: Section 5

1. When you hear, read, or observe something, how do you know what it means?

QUESTIONS: Section 5

2. What does "meaning" mean to you?

QUESTIONS: Section 5

3. Where does meaning "come from?"

QUESTIONS: Section 5

4. How do you understand what something "is"?

QUESTIONS: Section 5

5. Where do words come from?

QUESTIONS: Section 5

6. Where do symbols come from?

QUESTIONS: Section 5

7. Why do symbols change?

QUESTIONS: Section 5

8. What symbols does humanity have? For what reason? Why do they matter?

QUESTIONS: Section 5

9. What are some examples of good symbols and bad symbols?

QUESTIONS: Section 5

10. Are there symbols we could use but don't presently have?

QUESTIONS: Section 5

11. What bad symbols do we presently have that we would be better without?

Monsters exist, but they are too few in number to be truly dangerous. More dangerous are the common men, the functionaries ready to believe and to act without asking questions.

— PRIMO LEVI

QUESTIONS: Section 6

QUESTIONS: Section 6

1. Where does knowledge come from?

QUESTIONS: Section 6

2. Where do new ideas come from? How? Why?

QUESTIONS: Section 6

3. What do you think are some of humanity's most important ideas?

QUESTIONS: Section 6

4. Where did those ideas come from? How? Why?

QUESTIONS: Section 6

5. What, if anything should we do with those ideas? Why?

QUESTIONS: Section 6

6. What is a "good idea?" How do you know that it's good?

QUESTIONS: Section 6

7. Can a good idea become a bad idea? How? Why?

QUESTIONS: Section 6

8. Which of humanity's ideas should we reject? Why?

QUESTIONS: Section 6

9. How do you decide which ideas to reject?

QUESTIONS: Section 6

10. What is worth knowing? How do you decide?

QUESTIONS: Section 6

11. What are some ways to determine what is worth knowing?

QUESTIONS: Section 6

12. Who has the most important things to say today? Why?

QUESTIONS: Section 6

13. What are the dumbest and most dangerous ideas that are "popular" today?

QUESTIONS: Section 6

14. How does an idea become popular? Why are these ideas so "popular?"

QUESTIONS: Section 6

15. Where did these ideas originate?

The scientist is not a person who gives the right answers, he's one who asks the right questions.

— CLAUDE LEVI-STRAUSS

QUESTIONS: Section 7

QUESTIONS: Section 7

1. What is "progress"?

QUESTIONS: Section 7

2. What is "change"?

QUESTIONS: Section 7

3. What are the most obvious causes of change?

QUESTIONS: Section 7

4. What are the least obvious causes of change?

QUESTIONS: Section 7

5. What conditions are necessary in order for change to occur?

QUESTIONS: Section 7

6. What are the relationships between new ideas and change?

QUESTIONS: Section 7

7. Of the social changes currently going on, which should be considered, and which should be resisted? Why? How?

QUESTIONS: Section 7

8. How are these changes similar and/or different from other changes that have occurred before?

QUESTIONS: Section 7

9. What are the most important changes that have occurred in the past five years? Ten years? Twenty years? Fifty years?

QUESTIONS: Section 7

10. What will be the most important changes in the next year? The next decade?

QUESTIONS: Section 7

11. What are you basing your prediction on? Why do the changes matter?

QUESTIONS: Section 7

12. Of the changes that you predict will happen, which would you stop, if you could? Why?

QUESTIONS: Section 7

13. If you wanted to prevent one of the undesirable changes happening right now (pick one), how would you go about it?

QUESTIONS: Section 7

14. What potential consequences would you have to consider?

QUESTIONS: Section 7

15. Why is change so difficult at the individual and institutional level?

I would rather have questions that can't be answered than answers that can't be questioned.

— RICHARD FEYNMAN

QUESTIONS: Section 8

QUESTIONS: Section 8

1. What are the conditions necessary for life to survive?

QUESTIONS: Section 8

2. Which of these conditions are necessary for all life? For humans? For animals? For plants?

QUESTIONS: Section 8

3. What are the greatest threats to all forms of life? To humans? To animals? To plants?

QUESTIONS: Section 8

4. What strategies do living things use to survive? Which are unique to humans? To animals? To plants?

QUESTIONS: Section 8

4. What strategies do living things use to survive? Which are unique to humans? To animals? To plants?

QUESTIONS: Section 8

5. What human survival strategies are similar to, and/or different from, those of animals and plants?

QUESTIONS: Section 8

6. What survival strategies are enabled by human language that animals are incapable of developing?

QUESTIONS: Section 8

7. How might these human survival strategies be different without the use of language?

QUESTIONS: Section 8

8. Is human survival the same as thriving? Why or why not?

Courage doesn't happen when you have all the answers. It happens when you are ready to face the questions you have been avoiding your whole life.

— SHANNON L. ALDER

QUESTIONS: Section 9

QUESTIONS: Section 9

1. What other "languages" does humanity possess besides those consisting of words?

QUESTIONS: Section 9

2. What functions do those "other" languages serve? How and why did they originate?

QUESTIONS: Section 9

3. Can new and useful languages be invented? How might you begin?

QUESTIONS: Section 9

4. What would happen without mathematical languages? How would the world be different without them?

QUESTIONS: Section 9

5. What would humanity be unable to do without mathematical languages?

STAYING CONNECTED

- www.pk4l.substack.com
- www.linkedin.com/in/danielhagadorn
- @preparingkids4life
- @Inspiredlife360
- www.pinterest.com/vickilhagadorn
- dh@PK4L.com
- www.calendly.com/pk4l/30min

Preparing Kids for LIFE

PK4L

360° PARENTING

life = education without walls

www.PK4L.com

www.ingramcontent.com/pod-product-compliance
Lightning Source LLC
Chambersburg PA
CBHW060455300426
44113CB00016B/2599